Friends,

For forty-five years, the USA/Canada Lions Leadership Forum has been *Cultivating Leaders* to have a greater impact through-out all levels of our organization, our careers, and our local and global communities.

But as we've all experienced, so much has changed in the world around us. In our pursuit of making the world a bet-ter place through Lionism, it is imperative that we develop the skills and adapt our leadership strategies to address the opportunities and challenges that accompany rapid change. Michelle Ray's insights will help us do just that!

The USA/Canada Lions Leadership Forum is proud to be a part of the worldwide premiere of *Leading in Real Time: How to Drive Success in a Radically Changing World*. We believe this book will be a practical and inspirational resource to support our leadership journeys.

As the importance of leading in real time continues to emerge, thank you for investing in yourself and thank you for strengthening the future of Lions Clubs International!

In leadership, friendship, and service,

Wendy Cain

WENDY CAIN
General Chairperson
USA/Canada Lions Leadership Forum
Des Moines, Iowa
September 2021

Praise for *Leading in Real Time*

"*Leading in Real Time* is a must-read for all leaders and all those who motivate teams. As a beneficiary of Michelle Ray's wisdom, I'm so glad to see its essence captured in this informative and engaging book."

AIMÉE MEHER-HOMJI vice president, global talent acquisition, adidas

"Many write about leadership, but this book proves that Michelle Ray *lives* leadership. *Leading in Real Time* is both dynamically relevant and refreshingly daring. Michelle pulls no punches and offers specific insights into what leaders must be doing to advance their teams and goals in today's world."

SCOTT MCKAIN founder and CEO, Distinction Institute

"Brilliantly insightful, practical, and doable, this is *the best* leadership book I've read that captures the pain and the possibility of today's fluid world of work. Michelle Ray relates the wisdom of real-time leaders who adjust on the fly, nurture talent of all ages, and in the process become better leaders and people. If you seek to be a resilient, growth-minded leader, here is your guidebook."

EILEEN MCDARGH CEO, The Resiliency Group, and award-winning author

"*Leading in Real Time* knocks me out with its relevance, positive impact, and immediate value. It is an essential read for anyone who wants to be a better leader."

JOE CALLOWAY author of *The Leadership Mindset*

"Michelle Ray introduces immediately useful insights that we can put into action today to be the quality of leader people want, need, and deserve. Read it and reap."

SAM HORN CEO, Intrigue Agency, and author of *POP!* and *Tongue Fu!*

"Michelle Ray has magically transformed timeless leadership philosophies into present-day digestible and actionable concepts to enable and empower leaders in real time—and she's done so masterfully. Bravo!"

CODI SHEWAN speaker, consultant, and author of *Everyday Legacy*

"*Leading in Real Time* sheds new light on the profound obligations of contemporary leadership and the ways in which traditional leadership models are failing us. Any leader will benefit from the timely, practical, and optimistic advice it provides."

LIANE DAVEY *New York Times*–bestselling author of *You First* and *The Good Fight*

"*Leading in Real Time* contains many valuable lessons for today's and tomorrow's leaders if they want to remain relevant and, importantly, curious. Like a mixologist's well-made cocktail, it's really up to you what you take, make, and use for your future success."

FRANK PALMER chairman, Palmer Stamnes DDB

"*Leading in Real Time* showcases Michelle Ray's expertise in helping leaders to be ready, responsive, and relevant in an ever-changing business landscape. The book is a helpful and thorough guide to understanding what leadership involves today and how leaders must be willing to rethink everything so that they and their workforces thrive."

DENISE LEE YOHN author of *What Great Brands Do* and FUSION

"Michelle Ray is right on target with *Leading in Real Time*—and right on time! She communicates practical steps to become a better leader by uniting people from diverse backgrounds to work toward a common goal, camaraderie, and teamwork."

PAUL R. BLEDSOE past chairman, USA/Canada Lions Leadership Forum

"Michelle Ray's eight traits of real-time leadership represent breakthrough thinking and should be mandatory reading for all business executives."

JOSEPH SHERREN CSP, Canadian Speaking Hall of Famer and bestselling author of *iLead* and *Vitamin C for a Healthy Workplace*

"*Leading in Real Time* is a refreshing and right-now ethos for moving teams forward powerfully. The courage and presence required of a real-time leader is not for the faint of heart. The tools in this book are exceptional and will bring guidance to leaders at intense times. Michelle Ray's book is essential reading for any leader who wants the edge necessary in this new era of leadership."

KAREN JACOBSEN the GPS Girl

"Michelle Ray not only explains what it means to lead in real time, she gives you concrete steps to ensure you get there. Her entertaining and enlightening stories, real-life examples, and great questions will have you on the path to becoming a real-time leader. A must-read for any leader who wants to remain relevant and effective!"

RHONDA SCHARF Canadian Speaking Hall of Famer and bestselling author

"There is a turnover tsunami happening right now and Michelle Ray's brilliant book is your only hope of keeping your top talent— and attracting more. With original ideas, stories, practices, and principles on every page, this generous book is your field manual for leading in the new now."

DAVID NEWMAN CSP, author of *Do It! Marketing* and *Do It! Selling*

"In this meaningfully researched book, Michelle Ray brings into focus important events shaping the dynamics of an ever-evolving workplace. A must-read book for any leader who wants to motivate and lead a team forward."

JODY URQUHART author of *All Work & No Say . . . Ho, Hum Another Day*

"Michelle Ray delivers amazing rubber-to-the-road strategies for leaders to impact and engage their teams. Inspired leaders will learn that their interest and actions can shape the workforce of tomorrow. Invest your time in helping to chart that course and read this book."

TYLER HAYDEN CSP, author of more than twenty books

"*Leading in Real Time* is an insightful and reflective primer for business leaders as the world emerges from the COVID-19 pandemic and must grapple with new and difficult-to-predict challenges."

VICE ADMIRAL PETER JONES Royal Australian Navy (retired)

"*Leading in Real Time* is a must-read for all managers who want to successfully guide their business in an ever-changing world. It's loaded with examples that make you think in new ways, strategies to support diverse teams, and actionable ideas you can easily implement."

JENNIFER DARLING author of *Increase Your Leads with LinkedIn*

"Michelle Ray has captured what it takes to succeed on the frontlines of leadership in a world of upheaval and uncertainty. *Leading in Real Time* is loaded with real examples from real leaders who are just like you in their quests to build great, enduring organizations. Michelle goes a step further by giving you specific, actionable strategies to turn ideas into action."

RANDY PENNINGTON author of *Make Change Work* and *Results Rule!*

"Leadership style must evolve as the workforce changes. Today's workforce sees leadership as a position of service, not a position of power. *Leading in Real Time* should become the new gold standard for leadership now and in the future. The world will be all the better for it."

JEFFREY SHAW author of *The Self-Employed Life* and *LINGO*

LEADING

MICHELLE RAY

IN REAL TIME

How to Drive
Success in
a Radically
Changing World

PAGE TWO

Cataloguing in publication information is available
from Library and Archives Canada.
ISBN 978-1-77458-068-4 (paperback)
ISBN 978-1-77458-069-1 (ebook)

Page Two
pagetwo.com

Edited by Sarah Brohman
Copyedited by Rachel Ironstone
Proofread by Crissy Calhoun
Cover and interior design by Setareh Ashrafologhalai
Author photos by Lianne Cohen Photography

michelleray.com

Printed in Canada

TO MY GRANDCHILDREN, Cayden and Carrera; my nieces, Shayneh, Aliya, and Tova; and my nephew, Naftali. Your energy, unconditional love, and enthusiasm inspire me. You have reminded me of what it means to truly be in the moment. May you always be the leaders of your own lives. I love you all so much.

CONTENTS

INTRODUCTION
LEADING IN REAL TIME

___

MARCH 2020: It was a beautiful morning to fly home to Vancouver. Chelsea, a participant in the annual general meeting that I was hired to speak at, graciously offered to drop me off at the airport. At the time, the cases of COVID-19 in the region were almost nonexistent, so the attendees socialized as they normally would. The only sign that things were different was that small bottles of hand sanitizer were freely available for all delegates. However, no one was wearing a mask yet, as they weren't required or even recommended at the time.

On the flight home I reflected on my breakfast conversation with Chelsea the day before. Chelsea is an example of a brilliant hire by a global powerhouse who works closely with senior leaders and teams. Unfortunately, she had had an unpleasant encounter with a business leader that left her wondering about the future of her career with her current company. During a recent client briefing, Chelsea was told that her comments and perspectives were neither welcome nor appreciated. Even though Chelsea's suggestions were based on viable empirical evidence, the leader discounted her ideas. Her more senior male counterparts did not have the same experience when presenting their thoughts to this leader. When Chelsea countered by explaining how she had formulated her vision and strategies, she was disregarded yet again.

Chelsea sensed that the leader felt threatened by her knowledge and confidence, as well as her gender, but he seemed oblivious to the impact of his biases. The firm's client represented a sizable account, and yet in his refusal to acknowledge Chelsea's contributions, this leader risked losing both a valuable employee and potentially a client. His actions also had the potential to tarnish his organization's reputation as an outstanding service provider in a competitive multibillion-dollar industry.

Chelsea's disagreeable encounter with leadership made me think about how many leaders cling to outmoded ideas about how a leader is "supposed" to lead. They simply see no need to adjust how they lead their people even as the world changes around them, both inevitably, as it does with technology and shifts in the customer base, and sometimes cataclysmically, as it did with the COVID-19 pandemic.

Six days after returning from my trip, the World Health Organization (WHO) declared a pandemic. Little did I realize that my speaking engagement a week earlier would be my last in-person conference presentation for the rest of 2020. Like millions of people around the world, I soon found myself house-bound, watching my confirmed conference bookings evaporate in a slew of emails that flooded my inbox. Suddenly, I was staring at an empty calendar in a state of shock. My business had survived the economic meltdowns following 9/11 and the global financial crisis of late 2007 to mid-2009. But nothing could have prepared me for this unanticipated change of circumstances.

The irony of being a "leading through change" expert hit me. Massive disruption was taking place in real time. Was I ready? Were my clients ready? How would world and business leaders respond? When it became clear that my travel adventures would be on hold for an indeterminable period, I immersed myself in writing on this subject with a sense of urgency. And my observations on Chelsea's experience with leadership quite naturally became the springboard for the rest of this book.

As I had listened to Chelsea talk about her experience, her words brought to mind an expression used by my grandson, Cayden: "You're not the boss of me." The first time I heard him use it at the age of six, I was struck by his self-assured tone and was somewhat amused as he punctuated every sentence with the phrase during an entire weekend sleepover at our house.

In a curious way, Cayden's phrase captures the feeling of our new world of leadership because we now live in a work world where leaders and managers are no longer placed on a pedestal, revered, or feared by their workforce. We are in a new leadership age of parity, transparency, and diversity, and leaders cannot lead without adopting a collaborative, inclusive approach. My Gen Z grandson and granddaughter look to their teachers as role models who value the contribution of all students, regardless of background. Just like those Gen Z individuals who are a few years older and have already started their career journey, my grandchildren will carry their values of tolerance and understanding as part of their DNA into their working lives.

How leaders should lead has been a regular topic of discussion across multiple industries for decades, and many employers seek to educate their leaders specifically on this topic. But to my mind, if employees are to perceive leaders as trustworthy and effective, those leaders will first need to act like leaders in the *now*, or in *real time*, as we often refer to it today, rather than bosses who remains fixated on how they did things in the past. Today's business organizations must have a genuine intention to follow through and ensure that leaders expand and shift their thinking from fixed to open, and be ready to lead even when the answers aren't always at hand.

If there is one lesson to be learned from the events of 2020, it is this: expect the unexpected. The pandemic was a revelation for many leaders who suddenly understood the full meaning of being caught off guard in a moment where the present and the future collided with full force. You may be one of them: a leader thrust into real-time disruption on an unprecedented scale. Consider these three questions for a moment:

1   Are you ready to meet employees where they are and to hear their voices rising on a range of social issues that have also become workplace issues?

2   Can you be attuned to the needs of a workforce that looks to you for guidance but also respect their desire to carve out their own career path, whether that is as an entrepreneur, a remote worker, or a contractor?

3   Is your organization ready to answer the call regarding the digital revolution, AI, and other tech disruptors?

Throughout this book I will offer you strategies and ways to help you dig out your own answers and solutions to these questions. These strategies will help you to lead yourself, your team, and your organization. You will gain insights into the skills that are still essential for leaders and learn how to develop them so you can become an outstanding, dynamic, skilled real-time leader. At the end of each chapter, I have provided short

"Real-Time Takeaways" in case you want to quickly review the key points, as well as a "Real-Time Action Step." This action step is an activity designed to help you place the information in the chapter into practice immediately. Whether you are a tenured leader or recently began your leadership journey, you will learn how leadership has changed, and continues to do so, and why embracing change in the now is necessary if you are to be successful in the future.

One of the most gratifying experiences for me during the writing of this book was the opportunity to reconnect with clients and hear directly what the future of leadership means to them. All the leaders I interviewed for this book agreed that their leadership style has indeed changed out of necessity *and* desire. My research also revealed numerous examples of leaders who are currently breaking new ground in terms of empowering their workforce and redefining the roles therein, including their own.

These leaders understand that employees' expectations of leaders are dramatically different when compared to their past experiences at the helm of their organizations or departments. There were many common denominators among these leaders, but one lesson stood out above all: no matter what their industry or depth of experience, all identified the importance of not only becoming better leaders but better people. They genuinely love what they do and appreciate learning how to self-correct and admit mistakes. Self-awareness kickstarts the process of the evolved leader who can lead in real time and make authentic connections with the people they lead. Are you ready to become a real-time leader?

THE REAL-TIME LEADER

"Are you responding to the now or reacting to your past?"

RAMANA PEMMARAJU

LEADERS WILL always need to evolve and adapt without losing sight of what is right in front of them. But if today's leaders aren't prepared to lead and think differently about the world of work, they will fall behind. Not only do they need to expand their thinking around leadership, but they must be ready to lead in real time, whether that time is during a pandemic, generational change in the workforce, or fast-moving technological change. The future of leadership is being sculpted by employees and customers in a radically changing world. Leading in real time is what makes a leader future-ready, allowing them to better understand the expectations and aspirations of their employees and their customers.

Leaders who work in real time are doing what is needed to move the business strategy forward: they take care of their talent and make time for their people no matter what. They express a willingness to adapt to change in the customer arena while remaining cognizant of global events, such as the rise of employee activism, the influences of AI, and digital disruption. They are leaders like Frank Palmer.

I met Frank Palmer several years ago when he hired me to present to a group of advertising agency owners at their annual conference in Vancouver. Frank is an icon in his industry, renowned for growing Palmer Jarvis, one of the most successful agencies in North America, that was subsequently bought out by one of the largest media conglomerates in the world, the Omnicom Group. Through the merger, Frank was appointed the chairman and CEO of DDB Canada, a division of Omnicom. Frank had built his business from scratch, recruiting brilliant creative teams that were lauded for their work on many memorable, innovative advertising campaigns over the span of five decades. He is highly respected by his peers and clients as a maverick, a rule breaker, and relationship-builder. For Frank, a handshake remains the greatest bond of trust. His staff, clients, colleagues, and competitors alike greatly admire his passion and total commitment to people.

Frank believes that his industry, like numerous others, will continue to evolve. However, Frank is certain that big business must shift in order to survive. When he became part of a multinational corporation, Frank witnessed several trends that caused him to rethink his own career. Specifically, he experienced a lack of cooperation on the part of ownership regarding the need to take risks and reevaluate the benefits of working with independents on a greater scale. He made the decision in early 2019 to leave DDB for several reasons. Chief among them was his innate yearning to "get out of the prison," return to his entrepreneurial roots, and fully recapture his "joie de vivre." Frank believes that we are in the "age of the independent," explaining, "When you have an owner who wants to run a business the same way that he or she did in the last fifty years, you are going to fail. It's just a matter of time as the boat keeps taking on water. It's like the *Titanic* where we rearrange the deck chairs thinking things are the same."

It is difficult not to like Frank. He is a straight shooter who tells you what he thinks and inspires those around him to reach for the stars. For anyone who aspires to start their own enterprise, he believes that there has never been a better time than the present. What sets Frank apart from many leaders is his unshakable faith in himself and his capacity to embrace change. He is a nonconformist who recognizes that technology has made it possible for almost anyone to build their own brand and to be unafraid of revealing their talents in order to capitalize on opportunities.

In June 2020, Frank made the ad industry headlines again when he returned to DDB. I was curious to know what changed his mind and decided to ask him directly. He told me, not unsurprisingly, that he renewed the relationship with the agency on his own terms. Initially, he had received a call from Chuck Brymer, chairman of DDB Worldwide, asking him to come back "because we never should have let you go." Frank said that he would get back to him in a few days. When Chuck asked him why delay, he told him "you can't fix something that is already broken . . . when there is a lack of willingness to change. Let me think about it."

Several days later Frank made Chuck an offer: Frank would function as the company's local DDB office in Vancouver (where he lives) and pay the corporation a rights fee to do so. They agreed. Frank now has access to their brain trust, colleagues, industry research, and new business opportunities, but maintains his autonomy by having established a new entity, with his long-time friend and business partner, Bob Stamnes, known as Palmer Stamnes DDB.

FRANK EXEMPLIFIES all the traits of what I call a *real-time leader*: a leader who can adjust on the fly and coexist with an ever-changing workplace landscape that demands open-mindedness. He made a real-time decision to seize the moment, trust his gut, and create a situation that is beneficial for multiple parties. His energy and passion for people are magnetic. And his ongoing success is primarily due to his ability to recognize new realities while prioritizing the needs of his business, team, and clients.

Frank's repertoire of leadership skills will never become obsolete regardless of shifting demographics or digitization. The pace of technological change necessitates a fluid, flexible approach, a shift in thinking, and a readiness on the part of leaders to be the catalyst for ongoing transformation of their organizations. To meet the challenge, leaders need to be prepared to undertake an honest appraisal of their individual style by asking themselves whether they are effectively setting the vision for future success.

As the expectations of your workforce and of your customers evolve, it's the leader's responsibility to challenge the status quo, take the lead, and inspire employees to transcend self-imposed boundaries, both personal and organizational, to adapt and embrace new realities. The real-time leader raises the bar for all by employing a charismatic, daring, and open style.

A leader's capacity to project confidence and belief in others is showcased by their commitment to take a particular course of action and successfully motivate their team to come on board with that action. This singular outcome remains a fundamental aspect of successful leadership, no matter how many employees are under your watch. But the degree to which a leader is able to ignite a desire in their people to willingly change is directly related to the leader's strength of character, insight, awareness, and business savvy.

You can never diminish the influence and impact of great leadership throughout history. Outstanding leaders who inspire, motivate, flex, connect, collaborate, and remain open-minded are invaluable in the eyes of their workforces and key stakeholders. Current and future leaders who are keenly aware of their leadership responsibilities as well as business and economic realities will be poised for ongoing success. Leadership wisdom is evident among both tenured and newer leaders, but their success is not based upon age or years of experience. Rather, it is based on the lens that great leaders use to view the world.

The Challenge to Leadership

Since the dawn of time, leaders have been always ultimately responsible and accountable for the success or failure of their organizations. The old adage "it starts at the top" hasn't lost its relevance. However, the view from the top now looks vastly different, and astute leaders are constantly redesigning their systems and approaches accordingly.

The younger members of today's workforce see themselves as leaders, collaborators, change agents, and difference-makers who seek to create their own future. They want greater accountability from leaders and have clear values regarding causes that matter to them in anticipation of a bright future for themselves and the generations that follow.

Gone are the days of the autocratic leadership style. "Control freak" leaders find it difficult to accept that the workforce

Employees want to be on a level playing field. They want to be seen as your equal.

———

expects transparency, parity, and genuine connection. If leaders persist and expect teams to be mere followers, they will fail because employees want to be on a level playing field. They want to be seen as your equal and for you to be a real-time leader, not a "boss."

Throughout the course of my career, numerous leaders have lamented that younger generations are impatient and entitled. Interestingly, I haven't heard many say the same about their *own* journeys. Truth be told, there are leaders who feel that a leadership role was simply a given based on the efforts they made to climb the ladder. Or they may believe they were born to lead and their innate skills are sufficient for future success. However, you may be a leader who is discovering that your leadership journey has taken unexpected twists and turns. Accepting that you don't have all the answers may be unfamiliar, but it may need to become your new refrain.

Eric Hoffer, an American writer on social and political philosophy, once said, "In a world of change, the learners shall inherit the earth, while the learned shall find themselves perfectly suited for a world that no longer exists." Hoffer's timeless reflections and future predictions have indeed come true. If you want continued success as a leader, are you ready to embrace new standards and envision yourself as an eager student? Although a number of essential skills engrained early on in your leadership career will always be useful (see Chapter 3), you will likely find that what you thought you knew about leadership is never enough.

The biggest risk to organizations of every description is surprisingly easy to identify. But shockingly, many leaders would not recognize the major elephant in the room, whether that room happens to be the C-suite, the factory floor, a job interview room, a training facility, or a conference hall. If you were to ask leaders at all levels, "What issues are you focusing on to lead your organization successfully into the future?" the most obvious responses would likely include the following:

- Embracing change as the key to our survival.

- Acquiring the best and brightest talent to provide us with a competitive advantage.

- Budgeting for ongoing technological evolution and transformation while preparing our entire workforce with appropriate learning opportunities.

But I will tell you now that the number one reason that will derail every effort to successfully address these issues is a *fixed mindset*. When it comes to the failure of leadership nowadays, the key cause and challenge are pervading attitudes of intransigence, either conscious or unconscious. Sadly, it is mainly leaders who fail to address the urgent need to remove this critical roadblock.

If leaders want to mitigate the path to irrelevance or possible extinction, then harnessing broad-mindedness must take on a sense of urgency. Ignorance may be bliss, but it will eventually kill your business. To determine if you are perceived as broad-minded, ask any member of your workforce whether they see you as a leader who is open to hearing solutions or accepting new ideas. Or engage your people in 360-degree feedback that reveals your true biases regarding ageism (at either end of the spectrum), sexism, racial bias, and the list goes on.

Renowned research firms including Deloitte[1] and Gallup[2] have consistently demonstrated over four decades that a leader's values and actions play a significant role in determining whether talent are attracted to an employer. Despite all the evidence, numerous incidences of biases (recall Chelsea in the introduction) continue to be a major turnoff for many gifted individuals who have the potential to help your organization transform, transcend challenges, and remain economically viable.

Today's successful leaders leave their egos at the door and respect employees who may not just be younger but smarter, regardless of tenure or gender. This generational shift doesn't diminish the value of long-term employees who have contributed greatly to the success of a business. Great leaders place high value on contribution, loyalty, and experience, but real-time leaders recognize that the future workforce views leadership differently and they are willing to flow with change.

Eight Signs of a Real-Time Leader

So now that you know what the challenge to leadership is, how do you recognize a real-time leader in your organization?

As we saw with Frank's story, it is absolutely possible for a real-time leader to focus on both their people and their business. Real-time leaders must ensure that they make themselves available to their workforce, remaining attuned to their concerns, personal priorities, and business perspectives. They recognize that their words and actions have an immediate and long-term impact. Real-time leaders understand that their employees' priorities coexist with the needs of the organization, that both are vying for their personal attention.

The real-time leader demonstrates eight key traits that serve them well in their leadership role; the real-time leader is:

1 transformative
2 emotionally intelligent
3 open-minded
4 humble

5   exceptional at listening
6   optimistic
7   consistent and trustworthy
8   authentic

1. Transformative

Leaders who are transformative possess the capacity to truthfully assess their attitudes and behaviors. The capacity to lead into the future requires a heightened self-consciousness and an acute awareness of real-time events that are influencing business and the world of work (see Chapter 3).

In an overview of the 2020 Future of Leadership Global Executive Study and Research Report,[3] the authors note, "Today's trailblazing leaders increasingly recognize that in order to credibly transform their organizations, they must credibly transform themselves and their teams." The report identifies the behavioral traits of leaders that engage, inspire, and motivate the new workforce, as well as those traits that "erode" relationships and organizational culture. The latter traits include rigid top-down approaches that are still prevalent and that impede talent development at all levels. Real-time leaders who employ new behaviors with minimal delay and eliminate practices that impede the path to progress are poised to transform the challenges of navigating the future for themselves and their organizations.

The transformative leader intuitively understands when it is time to rethink and reevaluate their own approach. A leader's willingness to evolve with the times and stay in sync with the workforce, while giving them the freedom to thrive, exemplifies transformational leadership in action. Real-time leaders aren't invested in getting their teams to conform.

Rather, they embolden employees by providing support, while giving them room to create and collaborate.

2. Emotionally Intelligent

A leader's emotional intelligence, also known as the emotional quotient (EQ), has a profound impact on morale, productivity, and employee motivation. If you are in a leadership position, emotional intelligence is a prerequisite more than ever. Daniel Goleman's groundbreaking research[4] on the subject determined that a leader's emotional quotient accounted for 67 percent of the abilities necessary for superior leadership performance.

Human interaction is complicated, and even more so in the digital world. Individuals react differently to verbal and nonverbal cues and bring their respective histories, personal and professional, conscious and unconscious, into every social encounter. When addressing a team or an employee one-on-one, a leader who is cognizant of their words and actions, as well as how recipients interpret them, has likely honed their capacity for demonstrating empathy and self-awareness—these are essential skills that directly impact a leader's individual and team relationships. The importance of building trust and rapport in any work environment cannot be understated. In the grand scheme of things, a leader's emotional intelligence has a significant impact on shaping an organization's culture and its future.

3. Open-Minded

To lead effectively into the future, it's essential to acknowledge the talents of the people in your workforce that can propel your business vision forward. To do that, you need to sidestep your own biases. The degree to which an individual demonstrates receptivity toward new ideas indicates the difference between transactional and transformational leaders. A transactional leader may possess strong business acumen, a caring disposition, passion for their work, and strong organizational skills to manage the day-to-day needs of the organization. However, these characteristics don't necessarily mean that they are able to hear and receive suggestions regarding different approaches favorably or openly. Conversely, a transformational leader can transcend their own shortcomings and prejudices in order to recognize the value of ideas emanating from every level. Phoebe Dodds, a Gen Z entrepreneur based in Europe, and founder of content strategy company Buro155, described the need to maintain an open mind as follows:

> Don't discount the opinions of the lowest people in your company. Those are the ones who are closest to the source and are most likely to be forgotten. When I was an intern, decisions were made by cliques at the top. I prefer the idea of vertical integration, buddying systems within hierarchical structures, rather than people only talking to those who are at their level. This gives leaders the clearest image of what is happening in their business and how people feel. With all the options available, it's becoming less enticing for people to actually work in a company with hundreds of employees. Leaders need to be cognizant of these realities, otherwise they are not going to be able to retain top talent.

4. Humble

Practicing humility comes easily for leaders who are willing to admit they don't have all the answers or they have made a mistake. When a leader can accept that it is perfectly natural to be imperfect and detach from an ego-driven reaction in such circumstances, they become more approachable, likable—human! Many leaders consider humility to be a sign of weakness; however, in the eyes of their team, it is a highly attractive trait as it builds trust and an opportunity for greater connection.

There is a simple explanation for the lack of humility in leaders. The common paradigm of leadership in the past was based on a title, or holding a position of power that denotes authority and control over others, leaving little room for vulnerability and self-correction. A leader who exercises humility demonstrates transparency, resulting in greater opportunities to draw others closer. When challenging times arise, employees look to their leaders to act with sensitivity and to adopt an unpretentious style. This is especially crucial when organizational change is imminent and buy-in is paramount.

5. Exceptional at Listening

Listening and hearing are two critically different things, and there's nothing more off-putting than a leader who lacks the capacity to listen. A perceptive leader pays attention, talks less, and listens more. Interestingly, this opens up the door to some who may share a viewpoint that is entirely different from yours. In these situations, great listeners do not react. They recognize and acknowledge, either verbally or through positive nonverbal cues, that they have heard the other person. For example, you may reply, "Tell me more about your perspective," or "I would like to understand more about your point of view," even if you disagree. Respond by repeating what you heard, not sharing your reaction to what they said, and do this with genuine interest.

The concept of listening to understand, rather than to refute, as well as knowing the difference between hearing and listening benefits the real-time leader. It will serve you well when you need to respond quickly or make instantaneous decisions. Your capacity to genuinely listen is an attractive trait that goes a long way to bolstering your authenticity and credibility as a leader. It's worthwhile keeping in mind that the same letters that are in the word *listen* are also in the word *silent*. .

6. Optimistic

To suggest that an effective leader should be positive, upbeat, and optimistic might sound like an oversimplification. Nonetheless, it is important to reiterate the benefits. It is hard to imagine any team being inspired by a pessimist; a leader's positive persona is magnetic and critical for setting the tone in any work environment.

Brad Eshleman, former president, Western Stevedoring Group of Companies (now rebranded as Western Group), exudes confidence and positivity. Brad has tremendous responsibilities as the leader of a multibillion dollar enterprise that plays a significant role in the global transportation supply chain, yet he is fully present during every encounter. He is enthusiastic about his team, his company, and the future. His opening remarks during one of his company's leadership sessions that I attended immediately set the tone for a bright meeting and a bright future. He tempered realism with enthusiasm brilliantly while providing his "state of the nation" report. And he articulated his vision in a manner that generated ongoing excitement throughout the course of the day. His optimism and genuine approachability are traits that will always be well received by managers and teams alike. It was easy to understand why his team of senior leaders, or anyone who has the good fortune to connect with him, would immediately be drawn to his personality.

7. Consistent and Trustworthy

If you have worked with a leader who genuinely gets to know their people, sets and holds the standards, and follows through in their communication, you are fortunate. Empirical research in many sectors of industry confirms that consistent actions and behaviors on the part of leaders earn the respect and trust of individuals and teams alike. Yet a YPO Global Pulse survey released in January 2020[5] confirms the organizational ramifications of a persistent trust gap. The findings also show that leaders at the highest level find it challenging to build trust with teams and stakeholders, with the majority lacking a strategy to address the issue.

Although many leaders understand the strong correlation between how their teams perceive them and the impact of being a person of their word, they are still falling short. When a leader's attitudes and follow-through are inconsistent, they may become the weakest link—they are the problem instead of the solution. Without clarity and consistency, a leader's reputation is negatively impacted. The absence of clear and thoughtful communication has far-reaching consequences. Such actions slowly erode trust, morale, and engagement. Although there is no doubt that leaders feel the burden of internal and external pressures, responsibilities, and time constraints, attending to such fundamentals as getting to know their people and demonstrating genuine consideration for their needs goes a long way to achieving key business goals.

8. Authentic

Although strategic thinking and decision-making capabilities are essential leadership traits, the skills associated with the human side of leading others are equally if not more important. In times of constant flux, people need reassurance from their leaders. This is when a leader's ability to be relatable, authentic, and an outstanding communicator is key. Individual employees and teams need to know that leaders have the capacity to listen, to demonstrate genuine understanding regarding employees' fears or concerns. When they communicate authentically, leaders are able to connect with their teams on a deeper level and appreciate different points of view. By developing a greater understanding of others, they contribute to a collaborative space, enjoy the camaraderie of their colleagues, and sustain passion for their chosen vocation.

PEOPLE HAVE always looked to their leaders for certainty, support, and encouragement. These needs have become even more amplified during times of flux and anxiety, as leaders are called upon to step up as positive role models who can respond and draw upon firsthand experiences. By demonstrating these eight signs of a real-time leader, you can position yourself as helpful, genuine, available, and ready to adapt to new realities.

Real-Time Takeaways

- The number one challenge for real-time leaders is maintaining an open mindset.

- Lead with a willingness to adapt and change course quickly, accounting for the unexpected.

- Raise your level of awareness regarding real-time change that is happening internally and externally to better prepare yourself and your organization for new realities.

➤ Leaders who prioritize honing their people-building skills are better equipped during times of crisis and uncertainty. Your workforce wants to know that they can trust and connect with you.

Real-Time Action Step

Choose one of the eight real-time leader traits weekly for the next eight weeks and place it on your daily calendar. This visual reminder will bring the trait into your conscious awareness as soon as you review your daily schedule. Look for opportunities to practice that specific characteristic in real time.

THE WORKFORCE IS CHANGING AND SO MUST YOU

"When you're finished changing, you're finished."

BENJAMIN FRANKLIN

ANDREW SCOTT is a thirty-something business owner of multiple Pita Pit franchises and winner of a "40 under 40" award. Scott started his first franchise when he was twenty and was convinced that his drive to succeed and innate leadership abilities would take him where he wanted to go. But after only a year in business, Scott almost lost it all. He worked eighty to a hundred hours a week to salvage his dream and ensure that his father, who was his guarantor, would not lose his home.

Scott knew that he had to revise his entire leadership strategy to stay in business and keep his employees: "A different approach is to lead from their lens rather than your own. You need to be demonstrating at every point why something is important and how it will benefit them. Everything is instant, and you have to find a way to gear your leadership style toward that." Employers like Scott understand intuitively that their workforces need to see the meaning and mission behind all aspects of their jobs, whether they are mopping floors or mapping out complex AI or machine-learning applications. As he says, "People want to be part of something bigger than themselves. We were raised to believe that we could change the world. That we had something to offer. And maybe that was a message that prior generations never got... We were told we could do anything. And if you don't feel like you are changing the world, then you feel like you have failed."

Rather than micromanaging his team, Scott made it a priority to build trust and create systems that allowed his employees to progress and succeed without him spoon-feeding them. He realized that working 24/7 resulted in total burnout and a loss of the passion for the very thing he had worked so hard to create. He needed to let go and empower his workforce.

Scott's insights transformed not only his enterprise but also himself. He is a prime example of a real-time leader who understands that the changing landscape of business needs a different approach.

And the changing landscape of business is fast, furious, and complex.

Five Factors Changing the Business World

Recent world events, such as the COVID-19 pandemic, have magnified the sense of urgency for new thought leadership and methodologies. Leaders need to be exceptionally well prepared to expect the unexpected, to prioritize, and to be available for their teams like never before. For real-time leaders, transformation is not simply a goal but the process of taking action in the now to create immediate, relevant change that drives an organization forward.

In this section I'd like to focus on factors that real-time leaders, such as Andrew Scott, must acknowledge and work with if they want their businesses to be future-ready. Let's first assess the significant factors that are affecting your business, and then I'll offer strategies that will help you lead through them:

1 generational change

2 technological innovations, such as AI, blockchain, and machine learning

3 the gig economy

4 remote work

5 global interruptions, such as trade wars, recessions, or pandemics

The first four factors are somewhat entwined. For example, the 1970s and 1980s signaled a new era of technological transformation, morphing into the current digital age and an ongoing evolution and revolution in the workplace. At the same time, we witnessed the arrival of the knowledge economy. This dramatic shift has been defined as follows: "Society and economies are changing their reliance from the labor and manufacturing of products or goods to an economy that is more reliant on the production and reengineering of information into knowledge."[1] The rising dependence on intellectual capital is already redefining business, the composition of the workforce, and the relationships between leaders and their employees. However, the arrival of Generation Z as the first

For real-time leaders, transformation is not simply a goal but the process of taking action in the now.

true digital natives, who demand the flexibility of remote work and employment status, and the frenetic pace of technological transformation have only increased the sense of urgency that many industries are experiencing in their efforts to keep up.

The last factor is one that I think of as a global event of a limited duration, but one with the capacity to revolutionize how business is done, such as the COVID-19 pandemic.

Let's take a closer look at each in turn.

1. Generational Change

One of the more challenging aspects of leadership is acquiring a deeper insight into the values of the workforce. Leaders who are successful in building mutually rewarding professional relationships are able to suspend judgment, avoid generational labeling, and acknowledge worldviews different from their own.

Although generational differences have always existed, the implications of not appreciating or resolving these differences are more important now because we are in the era of the knowledge economy. The competition for human capital is fierce and demand for talent is an escalating leadership priority because there are five generations working together in today's workplace, an unprecedented occurrence. This is due in part to the increase in life expectancy over the past three decades and advances in the field of medical science that have resulted in a healthier population, allowing workers to choose to stay in the workforce longer. However, many individuals are also extending their careers due to economic necessity. In response to pressure from older generations who want to or are financially unable to retire, governments including those in Australia, South Korea, the US, Canada, the UK, Brazil, Spain, Poland, and the Philippines have abolished legislation regarding mandatory retirement.

When defining generational characteristics, it is difficult to avoid making generalizations. While we are all individuals with unique life experiences, and not everyone feels that they identify with or are represented by a specific definition of their generational cohort, it is widely recognized that people born within the same time span[2] can be seen as a collective with similar beliefs, values, and preferences. Although there are divergent opinions regarding the epochs for the current generations in the workplace, they are typically described as follows:

- Traditionalists, or the Silent Generation (born 1925–44)
- Baby boomers (born 1945–64)
- Generation X (born 1965–81)
- Generation Y, or millennials (born 1982–95)
- Generation Z (born 1996–2015)

The postwar generational group known as the boomers became infamous as the anti-establishment cohort that spoke out against the traditional values of their parents from the Silent Generation. Until the arrival of millennials (Gen Y), boomers garnered the most attention based on their size and massive economic and social impact. Although it is true that many boomers have already left the workforce, recent economic downturns have caused a large percentage of them to rethink retirement plans. Boomers remain a dominant part of the business landscape, but Generation Z, at 32 percent,[3] is now the largest cohort of the world's population.[4] The first generation to be labeled as such (with previous generations being named retroactively), boomers were originally referred to as "Generation X," a term first coined by Hungarian photographer Robert Capa who used it to describe the subjects of his photo essay, the young men and women growing up in the aftermath of World War II. Later, novelist Douglas Coupland used this label to refer to individuals who grew up in the 1970s and 1980s, and there the nomenclature stuck. The smallest cohort, Gen X is often described as the "sandwich generation" as they slot between boomers and millennials. However, many a Gen Xer would tell you that although they are small in number, they are mighty in stature, having learned resiliency skills as "latchkey kids," the first to be left on their own at home while both parents went to work.

Of the generations listed above, it is Generation Z who have an entirely different frame of reference to all things work-related. They have never known a world without the internet, smartphones, or social media. Their exposure to unparalleled educational opportunities and accessibility to technology are the ultimate game changers in any examination of the multi-generational workplace. But although Gen Z have only recently entered the workforce, they are experiencing their fair share of scrutiny and ridicule, despite the fact that they are influencing business, HR, and customer strategy at unprecedented levels, more so than their millennial predecessors.

As a result of the increasing influence of Gen Z, it is the real-time leader's responsibility to learn about the wants and needs of this new workforce. Here's how to tackle and manage this values shift.

Embrace the Entrepreneurial Spirit of Gen Z

The parents of most Gen Z, predominantly Gen Xers, were socialized in an era that saw a downturn in well-paying blue collar jobs, which sowed the seeds for their children to pursue higher education and reap the rewards. That means that Gen Z has become the most highly educated, savviest group of all the current generations entering the workforce to date. The individuals of Gen Z are now in demand for careers and jobs that were nonexistent three, five, or ten years ago.

First, know that relying on a minimum wage paycheck to pay off their student loans is simply not in Gen Z's DNA. Findings from a joint study by Entrepreneur and Internship.com that undertook research into the aspirations of Gen Z confirms this: 61 percent of high school students and 43 percent of college students would rather be an entrepreneur than an employee when they complete their studies.[5] Generation Z strongly believes that they are in charge of their own future, perhaps even more so than any other generation preceding them.

Real-time leaders recognize that they must adjust accordingly as they seek to hire and retain the talent of Gen Z. One example of how businesses and colleges are doing this is by identifying opportunities to provide career experience, mentoring, and lucrative internships for students who are in the formative stage of their career journeys. Take, for instance, UC Berkeley's center for young entrepreneurs at Haas School of Business and Columbia University's extraordinary Startup Lab. Begun in 2014, Columbia Startup Lab has raised billions in funds, founding over three thousand successful start-ups in the past decade. This is an outstanding example of an institution heightening their understanding of the digital native mindset to develop unique business partnerships.

Confront Your Personal Biases

How would you answer if a prospective employee said, "Tell me more about the way that your company is changing the world"?

My client Sarah was posed this question during a recent job interview with a prospective candidate, Sanjay. Sarah, a hotel owner, was looking to replace a recently retired operations manager. Sarah was impressed with Sanjay's confidence and resume, but she was taken aback when confronted by this question. When I asked her why she was surprised, Sarah told me she was unaccustomed to this kind of self-assurance, although she understood it to some degree. Sarah admitted that she felt out of her comfort zone when it came to leading millennials and Gen Zers and that she was quick to judge this generational cohort, citing her past hiring experiences. "They want a promotion almost as soon as they arrive," she said.

In fact, Sanjay's question is far from unusual as today's workforce wants to know that prospective employers are making a positive impact within their own communities and beyond. Deloitte's Global Millennial Survey[6] conducted during the 2020 pandemic highlights that despite being among the hardest hit financially, younger millennials and Gen Zers "see opportunities in the darkness and want to lead the change." True to form, Sanjay told Sarah that he felt strongly about working for a company that was invested in making the world a better place. The survey also highlights that both cohorts want to remain with an employer longer and are optimistic regarding the efforts that employers are making to align with their interests.

Whether you are reacting consciously or unconsciously, the time has come to recognize that judging your team or prospective talent based on their demographic can have a deleterious impact on your business. In challenging as well as in positive times, employer biases add additional, undue pressure on employer brand strategy as well as effective recruitment. Your organization cannot afford to ignore opportunities to recruit this new workforce.

Promote a Positive Workplace Culture

Building a healthy, congenial workplace culture must be a real-time leader's top organizational priority, with leadership

Building a healthy, congenial workplace culture must be a real-time leader's top organizational priority.

modeling exemplary attitudes and behaviors regarding their workforce. This is because, in addition to the external business consequences of generational stereotyping that I've discussed above, there are also internal ramifications for it, such as destabilizing your workplace culture. Jessica Kriegel, author of *Unfairly Labeled: How Your Workplace Can Benefit from Ditching Generational Stereotypes,*[7] uncovered "countless injustices" emanating from categorizing workers by specific demographic groups.

Take for example my client Mark, who happens to be a millennial. Mark is a brilliant salesperson for a company in the competitive agricultural business of manufacturing, supplying, and storing grain. He has a deep understanding of the industry as a third generation farmer, acquiring firsthand experience in his family's business. Mark has a degree in agricultural engineering and possesses extensive knowledge regarding current and future trends in his industry. He has many business contacts and is highly respected by his coworkers and clients. However, Mark feels that he does not have the complete trust of his employer when it comes to closing lucrative six- or seven-figure deals. The owner of the company will often step into the final phases of the selling process, isolating Mark from the conversation and client negotiations. He has even asked some of his colleagues whether he should grow a beard in order to be taken more seriously. Seriously?

Other non-millennial members of the sales team have not experienced the same level of intervention. Although Mark has expressed his concerns regarding age discrimination, his employer dismisses Mark's disquietude, downplaying his assessment of the situation. As a result, Mark is now questioning whether he will remain with the company. And many millennials are voicing sentiments similar to Mark's. Kriegel's research indicates that millennials are unfairly portrayed and have been singled out more than any other group in today's workforce.

Leaders take note: generational stereotyping and generalizing not only perpetuates disharmony between coworkers and managers, but it may also serve as grounds for litigation, with ramifications far greater than HR departments can manage.

Acknowledge the New Customer Base

Marketing to millennials and Gen Zers is a multitrillion dollar proposition. If your business is not positioned to promote and sell your services to these groups, to say you are missing out is an understatement. A fascinating report by Dynata[8] indicates that marketers will have a unique opportunity during and post COVID-19 to influence consumer behaviors; many companies have already established significant market share. The Dynata report also notes that with or without a crisis, these generational cohorts are of special interest, given their increasing spending power in the coming years and their ability to influence older generations.

It is the savvy organization that consistently anticipates, innovates, and recognizes customers' purchasing preferences. For younger cohorts in particular, increasing your digital capabilities[9] while demonstrating genuine, altruistic initiatives can help keep your brand relevant, attractive, and viable in their eyes. In addition, they are paying particular attention to and are influenced by the activities of companies[10] in relation to the environment, how they supported their own workers during the pandemic, and the stances CEOs have adopted on political issues.

By staying ahead of the technology curve and prioritizing your marketing strategies to capitalize on the spending power of millennials and Gen Z, you can position your organization for future success both as a consumer and as an employer brand of choice.

2. Technological Innovations

In 2015, Klaus Schwab, founder and executive chairman of the World Economic Forum, introduced the term *Fourth Industrial Revolution*,[11] and it became the focus of the 2016 World Economic Forum. He describes this current industrial revolution as one with "no historical precedent," evolving at incredible speed, with repercussions for virtually every industry and country. Schwab also states that "the breadth and depth of these changes herald the transformation of entire systems of production, management, and governance."

As workforce demographics continue to shift, paradigms regarding the nature of work are also changing. Man and machine can coexist. Mass production, essential for the global economy, requires critical partnerships between people and technology. Innovations such as AI, robotics, and machine learning promise to assist companies in gaining a competitive advantage, but only if leaders buy in wisely. Although you likely appreciate the ease of use that is often the end result of technology and expertise bringing great inventions to market, you also need a higher level of awareness regarding the positive impact of technology on your workforce and your enterprise.

In an article entitled "The 'How' of Transformation,"[12] the authors note that "regardless of the circumstances, real transformation happens only when a leadership team embraces the idea of holistic change in how the business operates— tackling all the factors that create value for an organization, including top line, bottom line, capital expenditures, and working capital."

Your perspective regarding technological change sets the tone for your entire organization. As a leader, how often have you asked yourself,

- How open-minded am I regarding digital transformation?

- Is my business future-ready?

- Will my business depend on technology in order to survive?

- How will new technologies positively impact attrition and retention?

- Does my organization have the leadership competencies to execute on technology?

Greg Hicks, CEO of Canadian Tire Corporation, is one example of a real-time leader who understands the significance of these questions and, more importantly, how to answer them. The timing of his first day in his current role was the morning after WHO declared the pandemic. Facing a myriad of challenges, Hicks turned the Canadian retail icon's e-commerce division into a massive success. Whether the pandemic served as the catalyst for essential improvement in this critical part of CTC's business, Hicks isn't certain. Nonetheless, his level of acuity regarding in-the-moment priorities is lauded externally and internally, by Martha Billes, CTC matriarch, as well as by senior executives and dealerships. Mr. Hicks's journal entries capture the executive's brightening mood in real time, such as this one: "Month of May CTR (click-through rates) sales is through the roof like nothing I have ever seen."[13]

Business organizations can ill afford to asphyxiate as a result of outmoded operations, so ongoing evaluation of your ROI in technology is paramount. One study reported[14] that close to one trillion dollars was wasted in an attempt to improve organizational efforts on digital capabilities. This was largely due to a lack of teamwork and a cohesive, collaborative approach as well as to the existence of antiquated systems to record the work being done.

There is no question that new technologies demand new strategies if organizations are to be successful in their efforts to stay relevant. Now is the critical time for real-time leaders to take the helm and guide their businesses and teams into the future. Kickstart this process by looking beyond your executive for direction, wisdom, and support.

Tap Into the Expertise of Your Workforce

In the new digital economy, leaders who are willing to tap into the knowledge and expertise of their workforce will position their organizations for ongoing success. A collaborative style of digital leadership will be essential, although evidence[15] suggests that many leaders are anxious and hypersensitive regarding fully embracing the transition.

Move Out of Your Comfort Zone

What does it take for leaders to move out of their comfort zones? If you want to be fully prepared to embrace the future and the inevitability of constant, rapid shifts in business and technology, you need to eliminate angst, control, and reactivity in your leadership style as much as possible. Instead, choose to embrace an all-inclusive, courageous, and transformative approach to every aspect of your operations as well as your work relationships. Gartner's research indicates that there will be significant implications for enterprises that lag in digital transformation, with 67 percent of leaders[16] saying that their companies will no longer remain competitive without championing it.

If you want to be fully prepared to embrace the future and the inevitability of constant, rapid shifts in business and technology, you need to eliminate angst, control, and reactivity in your leadership style as much as possible.

Reinvent, Re-skill, and Reimagine

Technological advances should make all business leaders think about reinventing themselves, re-skilling their workforce, and reimagining business possibilities. Keep in mind that there are leaders who are successfully leading their organizations through digital transformation, but they are not exclusively in the technology realm. Leaders at traditional, established enterprises have spearheaded significant reengineering of their processes by keeping their customers and talent at the top of mind. Companies such as Best Buy and Home Depot have been very successful[17] in their digital transformation investments, increasing market share and share price significantly. Internally, these companies have also ensured that their leaders at all levels are the right fit when it comes to developing a forward-looking culture.

Fully Buy Into Digital Innovation

CEOs report that there is a direct correlation between successful integration of digital technologies, customer growth, and profitability. They are also facing pressure[18] from their boards to adapt and keep their enterprises agile. But recent studies reported by Tech Republic indicate that the struggle to transform is real for many organizations. For digital innovations to be successful, real-time leaders must fully buy into the new technologies when appropriate for their businesses, recognizing that they are ultimately accountable for implementation.

Diversify Your Assets

Investment advisors use the term *diversify* to help clients allocate their capital investments in a variety of assets to prevent overexposure to risk; leaders need to think similarly in terms of asset management, that is, the successful blending of technological assets with human capital. The two can happily coexist[19] depending on how you set the direction. Developing and deploying complex technology requires talent, and talent cannot be replicated. You need both human and machine, or you risk supreme failure in your technological transformation initiatives.

Diversification can also be thought of in terms of re-skilling your workforce and transforming your culture. AI, for example, need not be viewed as a "job destroyer." There are certain tasks that cannot be automated, especially those that involve a high level of relational, personal connection. For example, technology can greatly assist healthcare practitioners, but it cannot substitute the high value patients place on empathy, honesty, and integrity. Also, as your organization continues to digitally evolve, doing so in tandem with cultural transformation makes for a stronger, more diverse team.

3. The Gig Economy

Boomers grew up in a period of postwar economic prosperity and usually remained loyal to their employers. However, the idea of having one job for life does not necessarily appeal to the newest generation of workers today, and it certainly is no longer the norm.[20] Research from Pearson's Global Learning Survey[21] found that the forty-year career has been replaced by lifelong learning and diverse career paths. Many jobs are becoming obsolete more quickly, and the individuals of Generation Z will likely find themselves working in jobs that haven't even been invented yet. The days of staying with one employer are fast fading into the past, and unless companies are willing to invest in their people emotionally and financially, the best and brightest will unashamedly seek opportunities elsewhere or will forge their own careers and businesses, leaving companies scrambling to replace people through headhunters or online recruitment sites.

In the last decade, organizations in the public and private sectors have made the shift to hire more contract workers. Today, the gig economy, also known as the sharing economy, is changing the face of organizations. Both parties are benefiting from this shift. Independent contractors can choose project-based or short-term work opportunities, allowing them the freedom to set their own hours and remuneration. And employers are realizing cost savings in terms of employment benefits and lowering overhead by hiring ad hoc.

The increase in freelance opportunities also affords companies the opportunity to explore nontraditional markets to acquire workers on a temporary basis, tapping into new sources of an innovative, creative talent pool. However, events such as economic downturns, and more recently the pandemic, have highlighted misconceptions regarding the benefits and demographic makeup of the gig economy. Having a side hustle is not a replacement for full-time work, and not always an option but a necessity for many workers. In an excellent *Washington Post* article,[22] the author notes that "not all gig work is created equal." Although gig work can provide independence and flexibility, economic uncertainty and a recessionary environment can quickly erode a worker's entrepreneurial aspirations and motivation.

Revamp Your Approach to Gig Workers

Real-time leaders see the value of creating ongoing employment opportunities for gig workers who work alongside their salaried workforce, based on their organizational needs.

Economic uncertainty caused by recession or global events, such as the pandemic, has resulted in companies reexamining their internal structures and long-established hiring protocols. Gartner reports[23] that 32 percent of companies are replacing full-time employees with contingent workers as a cost-saving measure. Supporting and valuing ongoing contract employees is one important way a leader can capture the benefits of the gig economy.

4. Remote Work

Home sweet home was the first location for labor long before the concept of remote work was popularized. In fact, working from home has been occurring for over a million years.[24]

During the Middle Ages as well as the industrial revolution, many people made their livelihoods by working from home. Fast forward from the Tupperware parties of the 1950s that spawned huge growth in homegrown businesses to the 1970s when engineer and physicist Jack Nilles pioneered the idea of telecommuting while working on a communications project for NASA. Nilles realized the benefits of performing technology-based work from a distance, that is, at a physical location outside of the traditional work environment, although not necessarily from home.

Working remotely has undergone a revolution in the last three to four decades. Those working remotely today may not be located in close proximity to their employer and could be in a different geographic area entirely. Research from Global Workplace Analytics indicates that the trend to working remotely is accelerating, with more than 80 percent of employees expressing interest to do so.[25]

The pandemic of 2020 highlighted the importance of mental wellness as it precipitated a fundamental shift in work arrangements from the top down. With millions of people working from home out of necessity rather than desire, both leaders and teams faced additional pressures, both personal and professional. People found themselves in unfamiliar circumstances, juggling family responsibilities with work priorities, and the need for increased compassion and consideration on the part of employers became essential. That need for compassion and consideration will likely continue to be a necessity as the workforce adjusts to a post-pandemic world.

Flex to Attract Talent

It is difficult to imagine that any industry will be left unscathed, financially and organizationally, when it comes to remote work, but what is clear is that companies that offer greater flexibility regarding work arrangements, including the opportunity to work remotely, are ideally placed to attract talent and increase overall job satisfaction.

Hire a Head of Remote Work

Many companies now recognize that flexibility regarding attracting new hires also extends to management. Businesses such as GitLab, an open source software firm that has been entirely remote since 2011, appointed Darren Murph as their head of remote in 2019.[26] Murph, who was the lead author on the GitLab Remote Playbook,[27] believes that "working remotely is a sea change, requiring a complete rearchitecting in how people think about work, where it happens, and when it happens."[28] Facebook, software company Okta, and others are either following suit or closely examining their need for the position. As Doron Melnick, national leader of people and change services at KPMG Canada puts it, there are benefits to "providing leadership at a time when it might not be obvious who should be leading."[29] Although some believe that the concept may be a short-lived post-pandemic fad, there is no question that remote work will continue to be the preference for a large number of employees and gig economy workers. And leaders at all levels will need to learn to provide a different kind of support to those who are not located in a traditional workspace.

5. Global Interruptions

All businesses will experience some kind of global marketplace interruption in their lifetime, whether that's a recession, a trade war, a new competitor, or an innovation that makes their product or service obsolete—and that kind of global interruption also includes the recent and unprecedented event of the COVID-19 pandemic.

The previous four factors are ongoing: generations change, technology develops, and where and how we work will continue to morph. But the pandemic will subside at some point, even though its effects may be long-lasting. This global event was still in process at the time of writing, and even when this book comes to print, the business terrain may well still be adapting, so it makes sense to use it here as an example.

For many leaders, the COVID-19 pandemic tested their faith and resilience as business organizations scrambled to adapt their game plans. Pandemic health imperatives required people to distance physically, but this mode of work was unfamiliar territory for the majority of the working population. For employees working from home already, doing so with their children or partners in the same space created additional challenges and stress. And leaders found themselves operating without a safety net as remote work became the norm for millions of people who had no choice but to stay home to stay safe. Leaders needed to trust their workforce who were out of sight but not out of mind.

As a result of the changes in work made necessary by the pandemic, some people will now prefer working remotely and it's possible a hybrid approach of at-home and in-office work will materialize. There is already evidence to show that this will be the new norm for some companies and industries. Some organizations like Twitter and Square publicly declared that their employees could choose to work from home forever, while others, such as Apple, requested only specific teams return to the office. But despite the significant disruption in employment that the pandemic created, there is compelling evidence of a shortage of technical[30] and other professionals[31] whose skills continue to be in demand. When sectors struggle with decisions to furlough staff because a global event like the pandemic demands it, leaders must consider the long-term cost implications[32] of layoffs as they simultaneously plan for recovery and the need to rehire.

Even though the pandemic has accelerated the effects of certain factors discussed in this chapter, no doubt there will be other global disruptions yet to be imagined. Here are four ways that real-time leaders can respond to the effects of most global disruptions:

1 **Take a fluid approach.** In the midst of a global disruption, every organization experiences a different impact on their business as usual. But the only viable solution to maintaining operations is for leaders to first adopt a flexible position. Although you may have to lay off workers or shut down operations either temporarily or permanently, maintaining a readiness to shift, respond, and remain positive during a state of flux is imperative for real-time leaders. Jennifer Wong, president and COO of Aritzia, a highly successful

women's fashion brand, intuitively understood what it took to guide her team and the business as soon as the pandemic hit. Despite the temporary store closures, the company was already ideally positioned to pivot, implementing safety protocols and adopting new processes at their distribution centers to continue fulfilling online orders. As reported in the *Globe and Mail*, Aritzia "did not lay off any staff, shifting many to help with e-commerce and call center operations. In the first few months of the pandemic [the company's] e-commerce revenue surged by more than 150% over fiscal 2020."[33]

2   **Re-skill your workforce.** Sometimes an unexpected benefit of this kind of business interruption is the realization that specific skill sets are now in demand. Organizations have a growing need for knowledge through data analytics and business intelligence to help make informed decisions and glean insights that assist with crisis management and business continuity. Take advantage of the opportunities now available to you and your business to either re-skill your workforce in these areas or to acquire new talent.

3   **Support the use of technology.** Real-time leaders must be alert to the possibilities of new technologies that may affect their businesses in the future and be ready to shift and support as appropriate. During the 2020 pandemic, businesses curtailed travel and relied upon online portals such as Zoom, Microsoft Teams, and Webex to stay in touch with employees and customers. However, it is highly likely that the uptake of these tools will become more permanent due to cost savings and ease of use. Leaders and teams are also using these applications for educational purposes as they reconfigure learning and professional development opportunities.

4   **Prioritize relationships.** Leaders are recognizing the value
of being more transparent and accessible, and employees
are seeing leaders in a different light as a result. This crisis
reinforced that no matter the circumstances, people still
crave social interaction and have a deeper appreciation
for the coexistence of high tech and high touch. Despite
the restraints of lockdowns and social isolation during
the COVID-19 pandemic, CEOs reported[34] that this crisis helped them forge closer working relationships. The
enforced slowdown afforded them more time to connect
with their employees on a personal level.

THE PROLIFERATION of new technologies, change in work
styles, and the emergence of a new generation entering
the workforce provides organizations with fresh ideas and
opportunities to reinvent themselves. As the business world
continues to adapt and change to the moving landscape, your
objective as a real-time leader is to put the following three Rs
into action.

1   **Rethink.** Since remote work will continue to be a sought-
after alternative as employees and managers seek greater
work/life integration, you will need to factor this into your
business plans. As well, the shift from face-to-face to virtual meetings will continue to be a viable option. Whether
your team is working in an office or a factory, reconfiguring
the workspace will continue to be a work-in-progress. Keeping multigenerational teams engaged and inspired in the
absence of in-person connection will also be an ongoing
top-of-mind priority if you want to preserve your company culture and maintain camaraderie. Review how you
are reconfiguring your hiring and retention strategies to
meet your organization's immediate needs. Rethinking and

synchronizing your approach to your HR priorities (p. 174) are part of being an effective real-time leader.

2 **Respond.** The prophetic words of Greek philosopher Heraclitus, "there is nothing permanent except change," ought to be the catch-cry for every real-time leader. Unfortunately, the comfort of remaining in the status quo may be attractive for some leaders unless they are jolted out of this state by necessity. Instead of fighting the inevitability of change, responding to it is the far better choice. The process of thoughtfully assessing change is a skill, whether the change occurs unexpectedly or by design. The risky alternative is choosing to operate in reactivity or "firefighting" mode. Consider that many organizations were aware that huge numbers of their boomer workforce would eventually retire. Yet they operated without a succession or recruitment plan to replace the loss of knowledge and experience. Real-time leaders are aware of changing workforce demographics, constantly evaluating skill gaps, talent shortages, and people movement to safeguard the future of their enterprises.

3 **Rebound.** There is little doubt that workplaces will continue to evolve, and change will always occur, expectedly or otherwise. Confidently charting your course through ongoing change is an integral part of real-time leadership, even if change creates a setback or the challenge appears to be insurmountable. Fear is the emotion that can stop you in your tracks. Your best option is to look to the future with positive anticipation by choosing to rebound from the workplace trends over which you have no control and focus on what you can.

Real-Time Takeaways

- Real-time leaders need to be exceptionally well prepared as they confront the ever-evolving business landscape. Expect the unexpected and be available for your teams like never before.

- Generation Z is entering the workforce but with different expectations and demands. If you want to attract and retain this talented cohort, be open, flexible, and willing to listen.

- Embrace technological innovations wisely. Be ready to remove archaic systems and practices that impinge on progress and possibilities.

- Flexible work arrangements are the new norm. Your team may comprise gig workers as well as salaried employees, and this balance should be struck based on the immediate needs of your organization. It's important to value the output of gig workers and provide feedback as you would for your salaried employees.

- Work styles and locations will evolve as remote work becomes more integrated in how we do business.

Real-Time Action Step

Review the five changes outlined in this chapter and choose one that represents the greatest challenge in your workplace. Where could you make the most immediate impact in terms of how you lead your organization? And what would be one idea that you could implement to meet the challenge in a proactive, positive manner?

REAL-TIME LEADERS ARE READY AND RELEVANT

"I stay ready so I don't have to get ready."

CONOR MCGREGOR

SIGNIFICANT SOCIOECONOMIC events as well as how you identify yourself in terms of demographics may have influenced your leadership style on a conscious and unconscious level. As a boomer, my recollection of and experiences with bosses was a mixed bag. I placed a few of them on a pedestal while others remain memorable for all the wrong reasons. Unfortunately, many of you likely share my sentiments regardless of your age. The mediocre leaders appear to far outnumber the great ones.

You may still be seeking a role model, or you may have lost touch with your reason for choosing to become a leader. As more eyes are on a leader's character, actions, and direction, recognizing the significance of your decision to become or remain a leader is more important than ever. If you are passionate about remaining effective, relevant, and ready to evolve, now is the time to ask yourself why and how you became a leader, just as Aimée Meher-Homji did.

When I first met Aimée she was the VP of talent acquisition at Sodexo USA. Aimée is now the VP of global talent acquisition at adidas and is a renowned global HR leader. While she was at Sodexo, I worked with Aimée's talent acquisition leadership team, who are all virtual employees, responsible for the hiring and placement of thousands of managers and staff in schools, universities, hospitals, senior living communities, and other key industries. When I asked Aimée about her leadership philosophy, this is what she shared with me.

> Leaders need to thoughtfully reprioritize the time we give and how we give it. Being transparent, authentic, available, and vulnerable. I make sure when I am meeting with them or having a motivational conversation, I will relay my own vulnerabilities. It is important that I relate to them on a personal level. I am constantly sharing examples in my career where I had a misstep or a challenge and where I had specific learnings. It's not that my experience trumps theirs. It's about showing them that I am a senior leader and I, too, have navigated challenges. I still have learnings and things to go through. I believe that there is a tendency for senior leaders in general to get so caught up in delivering the message, moving things along, or keeping people motivated that you forget you are talking at them rather than talking to them... that you are talking to them from a podium rather than sitting in the trenches with them.

Aimée understands at a deep level that it is a priority to connect with her team so she can be relevant and meaningful. While at Sodexo, she held weekly meetings with her leadership team and town halls with her entry-level recruiters, who attended without their managers so they could speak freely. Her genuine interest in people and her desire to lead and make a difference are foundational attributes that contribute to Aimée's ongoing success. Championing diversity and inclusion is of paramount importance to her; she knows that there are leaders who possess a heightened awareness of inclusivity, who are respected and needed. And she believes in "leaders at all levels," regardless of whether an individual has direct reports, and that being open to learning how to lead is paramount for those who either aspire to or are in a leadership role.

Why Are You a Leader?

As a leader myself, and a *student* of leadership for more than thirty years, why people become leaders is a subject that has fascinated me continually. Some people choose to become leaders while others find themselves in a leadership role unexpectedly and stay in place, despite knowing that this esteemed vocation was the wrong choice for them. In the current climate of ongoing digital disruption and transformation, when a company has the wrong leaders in place at the wrong time, this will undeniably prove to be a costly and potentially irrevocable mistake.

Your initial motivation to become a leader may have served you well in the past. But is it still relevant? This is a key question if you want to remain effective and successful for years to come. If you have been in a leadership role for many years, you have no doubt witnessed staggering change in every aspect of business and the world of work. Technological innovation and the digitization of everything have been the greatest drivers of change. If you stepped into your role within the last five to ten years, you have also witnessed ongoing transformation, occurring at an ever faster pace.

I became a leader because I was enamored with the opportunity, but I seriously underestimated the level of responsibility and challenge I would face. I liked the idea of advancing my career, although there were many occasions where I felt out of my depth and didn't have anyone to turn to for help. Times have changed. Becoming a leader without knowing your why has ramifications that go way beyond yourself.

Consider the following catalysts and identify if any apply to why you became a leader:

- I was good at my original job.

- Becoming a leader was a natural progression in my career plan.

- The money and package were too good to pass up.

- I was promoted.

- I liked having the title.

- It was a matter of happenstance.

- I wanted to make a difference.

- Others convinced me that I had it in me.

If you were motivated by title, ego, remuneration, opportunity to use your skill set, or an altruistic reason, think about what it takes to effectively lead in today's business environment. It is highly likely that your responsibilities, pressures, and priorities have changed greatly, along with the composition of your workforce. Do you still have what it takes to rise to the challenge and answer the call? And do you have the energy as well as the willingness to continue leading?

Leaders need to
be future-ready
if they are going
to lead in real time.

━━━━━━━━━━

Whatever the motivators were that inspired you to become a leader, the cold hard facts remain: leaders need to be future-ready if they are going to lead in real time. This may appear to be paradoxical, but leaders must possess the competencies required to be successful in an ever-changing business environment. Leaders, as a collective, must be confident, insightful, flexible, and willing to lead a workforce that continues to evolve. And people, not technology, will continue to drive innovation and results.

Four Essential Skills for the Real-Time Leader

The time is now for leaders to be asking why they want and continue to lead. As you ponder this question, recognize that there is a big difference between answering the call "people need great leadership" and being willing and ready to step up to do so. Although it is admirable to have the desire to lead, it is important to be truthful with yourself while you consider whether you have the following four essential skill sets and strategies needed to lead into the future.

1. Interpersonal Communication Skills

Leaders are expected to be competent communicators, and no one is immune from close scrutiny, criticism, or ridicule. As a result, the significance of acquiring interpersonal communication competencies is greater than ever. Today, a leader's shortcomings as well as strengths are instantly judged. Real-time leaders who are adept at creating authentic connection understand that their success is underscored by harnessing exceptional people skills.

If you are experiencing difficulty in this arena, you may want to rethink your approach. And it starts with an honest appraisal of your current situation. Brett's story below is a good illustration of self-awareness and understanding one's short-comings, as well as the willingness to make improvements.

During a full-day presentation for a small group of leaders, the topic of interpersonal communication was earmarked for discussion following lunch. As the attendees left the room for the break, one participant named Brett stayed behind and asked, "What should I do if I don't like people?" I took a deep breath while I quickly gathered my thoughts and said, "Thank you for asking. Tell me a bit more about why you became a leader."

Brett paused briefly and replied, "I took the lead on a major project. I'm a technical guy as were the rest of my team. But the people dynamics were a real challenge. The company promoted me because the project was a success, and I accepted. It's the people part that I find the most difficult."

Several thoughts occurred to me as I listened to Brett's answer. First, he took the initiative on his project, which was commendable. Second, he admitted that he found the people management side difficult. I also appreciated his candor—humility is a positive leadership quality. The admission that a person accepted the promotion to a leadership position is a motivator for becoming a leader. But it does not necessarily imply that the person has the desire, the skills, or the attributes necessary to effectively lead others.

Then I asked Brett about his work history prior to becoming a team leader. He had been in aviation for eight years, starting as a project analyst on a small team. He would occasionally interact with his colleagues, who were equally focused on data analysis and project documentation. Brett mentioned that although his team relationships were cordial and individual responsibilities were understood, the majority of the team kept to themselves. He appreciated that he wasn't expected to socialize with them, nor was he ultimately accountable for the team's success.

As Brett found himself becoming more immersed in the relational aspects of leadership, he became more uncomfortable and he realized that his real struggle was internal. When offered the promotion, he hadn't given much thought to leadership in terms of interpersonal skills, and he wasn't prepared for the people side of his new role. He was faced with the choice between acquiring new interpersonal communication skills, continuing to feel out of his depth, or leaving his position. We had a brief but frank conversation about his dilemma. I admired his honesty and explained that if he had a strong desire to grow as a leader, his first step involved understanding that real-time leaders need to be great communicators.

Brett's story is not uncommon. Many leaders are promoted based on their success in a different capacity. Some jump at the opportunity while others approach the challenge with trepidation. When an individual like Brett feels discomfort, they may not always speak up, and this is the core problem. When a leader's ego gets in the way, there are potential ramifications for the team and the organization that may not be immediately apparent.

Can a leopard change his spots? Absolutely! However, when a leader is floundering regarding the capacity to effectively communicate and build relationships, or they consider it beneath their dignity to make improvements, the consequences can be disastrous. The following solutions I've suggested are ones I shared with Brett should he decide to earnestly pursue his leadership career. None of these is a quick fix, but I recommend them to all leaders who are keen and willing to learn or strengthen their leadership skill set.

Hire a Coach or Work with a Mentor

Real-time moments are part of lifelong learning, a journey that is never-ending. One of the best ways to improve your repertoire of interpersonal skills (or to assist with leadership proficiency) is to hire a coach or work closely with a mentor. Soliciting feedback and being able to discuss specific areas that you wish to improve will boost your confidence. Seek out someone that you trust or ask your peers for recommendations, and be ready to disclose your challenges and vulnerabilities.

Great leaders evolve by constantly learning. They avail themselves of a trusted advisor, or group of advisors, and often those conversations are spontaneous. Sometimes these advisors are their employees. If you truly wish to know whether you are hitting the mark, ask them for input and be ready for their responses as you will be pushed out of your comfort zone. If there is a high level of trust between you and your employees, they should provide a candid assessment of their experiences with you and will appreciate that you asked.

Ask More, Tell Less

Although some leaders still prefer an autocratic style, others recognize that their success today and in the future is dependent upon reevaluating their relationship interactions. Adopting a more inclusive style *can* be a win-win! For example, you can make simple changes, such as asking more and telling less. When you get into the habit of asking others what they think and how they would go about solving a particular challenge, you are positioning yourself for growth. Not only may your team members offer an alternative or a series of options that might be better than any you can come up with, but you also become increasingly adept at leading more collaboratively.

Study and Model Best Practices

The spiritual axiom "take what you want and leave the rest" applies in leadership. When you witness others giving their undivided attention to a leader in a formal or informal setting, focus on that leader's mannerisms and words and the receptivity of their audience. Although your style may be different, you will certainly gain invaluable insights into how and why these leaders are connecting, or not. Evaluate the energy exchange and notice whether people are smiling, participating, and contributing to the conversation.

Real-time leaders understand that there are different modalities with which to captivate their listeners and they adjust accordingly. All conversations comprise a sender and a receiver. It is the *sender*'s responsibility to be clear, rather than the receiver's responsibility to decipher the meaning of their words. For example, if you are a baby boomer or Gen X leader engaging with Gen Z (or vice versa), the onus of understanding your recipient's needs lies with you, the sender. If you aren't sure about the best way to get your message across (or where and how to deliver it), just ask.

When you increase your awareness regarding others' preferences, you demonstrate respect as well as flexibility. Whatever industry you find yourself in, understanding and prioritizing human contact based on what an individual needs from you in the here and now will continue to be one of your greatest leadership assets.

2. An Inclusive and Collaborative Style

Today's most intuitive leaders realize that their success depends upon helping others be successful. A leader who possesses an all-embracing approach to problem solving has grasped the value of seeking out and acting upon the collective brain trust. The trend toward cross functional teams and shared knowledge will continue to accelerate as organizations incorporate new technologies and continue to innovate. The collaborative process isn't static, and it is no longer enough for enterprises to simply keep up or be caught off guard by unexpected disruption. The enlightened leader is always seeking fresh ideas, new approaches, and divergent opinions.

People, not processes or technologies, will ultimately drive your competitive advantage. By tapping into the diverse experiences and wisdom of your team as a whole, you will be ideally prepared to embrace future opportunities. Remember, your current and future workforce comprises free-thinkers, freelancers, and entrepreneurs who expect to be engaged in and contribute to your leadership conversations, so it is important to ensure that their intellect and ingenuity are genuinely appreciated and included when planning the future direction of your organization.

Regardless of whether you work in business, not-for-profit, or government, surround yourself with brilliant minds who know more than you do to make your systems work optimally. There isn't an organization today that isn't grappling with complexity and myriad challenges to improve efficiencies. Time and again leaders have shared their struggles of keeping up with technology, identifying their unique point of difference, gaining the edge over their competitors, satisfying their customers, and maintaining an engaged workforce. And the struggle continues for obvious reasons associated with the demands of a leadership role. However, these struggles are also self-inflicted, showing up in a reluctance to let go of control and enlist the support of others in the process.

Real-time leaders communicate, connect, and collaborate with their workforce and understand they cannot achieve business goals in isolation. What follows are some ways to do that.

Acknowledge Your Limitations

When I first met Michael Campbell, this manager of more than two hundred custodial staff at Dalhousie University was sharing his success story of zero long-term work injuries among his staff with an audience of leaders attending an annual safety conference. His achievement was unprecedented in the history of his workplace. Even more remarkable was the fact that the number remained at zero for five consecutive years. The key to Michael's success was that he was willing to acknowledge what he didn't know and then surround himself with people who had the answers or knew where to find them.

Prior to his arrival at Dalhousie, many facility workers were repeatedly injured. To address this, Michael knew that he had to change the culture, and to do that he needed to change mindsets. He realized that there were partnership opportunities sitting on his doorstep that could help him. So he joined forces with students of the Occupational Therapy School as well as an external organization that helps immigrants settle in their new country, as many of his workers did not speak English. He sought the opinions of his team members, and all the groups worked together to get the safety messages across to staff. Along the way, Michael developed a program that is now sought out by other universities and businesses due to its huge success.

Michael's success demonstrates the power of collaboration and the mindset of a real-time leader. He envisioned numerous benefits for his own workforce and the community at large by adopting a multi-pronged approach to problem solving, without struggling to do it all himself.

Agility Plus Strategy Equals Vision

In addition to being collaborative, the ability to be agile and responsive to ongoing disruption is also a prerequisite if you aspire to be a real-time leader. These competencies go hand in hand with establishing the long-term direction as well as the distinctive core activities of your organization. What separates leaders whose career paths remain relatively static from those who progress is the ability to take a wider view of their enterprise. Those who progress understand where their organization is positioned in relation to competitors and can articulate a set of unique and specific goals.

Leaders who set company vision recognize that their strategy cannot be realized without the participation of their teams. They inspire people to buy into the vision while accepting that the journey involves making adjustments while meeting challenges head-on. And recalibrating in the face of the unexpected is a crucial piece of this process.

Run It Like You Own It

At the beginning of 2020, one of my clients in the global transportation sector brought its leadership team together for their annual meeting and strategic planning session. The company's president, Brad Eshleman, whom I introduced as a shining example of optimism in Chapter 1, explained that their meeting theme, *Line of Sight*, was specifically chosen to give the entire management team, including the superintendents, clarity on the direction of the corporation, direction that would flow out to all employees.

Brad's leadership style resonates with employees at every level. He clearly recognizes that his entire team are responsible not just for their individual performance but also the

The ability to be agile and responsive to ongoing disruption is also a prerequisite if you aspire to be a real-time leader.

———

organization as a whole. His highly effective relationship-building skills illustrate the panache one needs for success at the most senior level.

Both the meeting and theme reinforced the importance of every business unit and team within the company vis-à-vis their respective contributions. In addition, the meeting served as an opportunity for leaders to hear from their peers and gain a deeper understanding of the challenges and opportunities that lay ahead. Serving customers with a standard of excellence, supporting and leading their workforce, remaining financially viable, and maintaining impeccable standards of safety were the key pillars identified as ongoing drivers for success.

As I listened to the presentations from Brad, the executive team, and all divisional leaders, their passion and commitment to the business was clear. Each leader had a clearly defined goal for their division and was acutely aware of their clients' priorities and unique circumstances. The environment, terms of trade, weather conditions, and economy greatly influenced their clients' profit margins. As a result, all business units agreed that maintaining strong relationships while helping their clients navigate uncertainty and disruption was directly connected to realizing their own strategic vision.

Like many organizations, the company was subsequently impacted by the global pandemic. I followed up with Brad several months after the company meeting to ask about the status of their strategic planning and goal-setting process in the midst of the pandemic. He proudly reported the following:

> COVID-19 was certainly a disruptor and a big concern for implementation. But an interesting thing happened without prompting or follow-up—we've just reviewed our Strategic Objectives with each business unit and department, and they have completed it all! The goals we set in our planning sessions

have been cascaded down to all of our employees. Putting everyone on the same page, heading in the same direction. We were pleased to see that empowering our business unit leaders to run their divisions drives accountability even in a pandemic. We encourage our leaders to "run it like you own it." You have the autonomy to run your division like you own it, and we are there to help. That's our approach. And if there are issues, we talk about it and figure out how we deal with it.

3. Champion Change

Leaders who have a propensity for anticipating change (or, dare I suggest, for welcoming it) are acutely aware of the need to stay ahead of the curve. To go a step further, the true champions of change are those who are at the forefront of disruption and innovation. They *create* change.

Real-time leaders realize that non-complacency often goes hand in hand with success. They are trendsetters, unafraid to shake up the status quo and eager to be first to market with their products and services. The exponential growth in technology will continue accelerating and so the pressure on leaders and organizations to constantly evolve has never been greater.

Despite all the evidence, pushback from leadership against essential change initiatives continues to be the number one reason for the collapse of many organizations in almost every sector imaginable. If you were to trace the path to extinction of previously renowned entities and brands, you would invariably find that the root cause leading to their demise started at the top. It wasn't a case of making the wrong move; it was failure on the part of leaders to make *any* move.

There is enormous risk to the future of a company when its leaders are more comfortable building walls instead of bridges.

Not only do they risk their own downfall, but they also place their entire organization, workforce, and customer base in jeopardy. The fear of change is greater than the potential of tomorrow.

Such was the case for one of my clients, a not-for-profit organization whose leadership was made up of a majority who were clinging desperately to past glories. Only a handful of the executive team, including the CEO, felt differently regarding the path forward. They saw the writing on the wall but were increasingly frustrated at almost every turn.

Like many businesses and public sector departments grappling with attrition due to retirements, the organization's membership base was aging. Their visions and values were clearly articulated, and the work of their members had made a difference in the lives of thousands of people around the world; however, their board of directors were fiercely divided regarding strategies to attract, recruit, and involve a younger population. Leaders at the area, chapter, and local levels (all volunteers) were burned out and frustrated.

Although they realized that change was inevitable for their organization's survival, the collective desire and momentum needed to make the necessary shifts was too big a mountain to climb. So their CEO, June, hired me to reengage their leaders, provide a reality check, and facilitate a process for the entire organization to buy into change. What follows are the solutions that I recommend as a way for real-time leaders to become champions of change.

Exercise Empathy

Leaders who practice thoughtfulness, sensitivity, and exceptional listening skills regarding the emotional side of change are generally more successful when implementing next steps.

As part of my process to help June's leaders and members, digging into the reasons for resistance to change was the first step. Mary, a long-term member and area leader based in South Africa, shared a story that I have never forgotten, as it typified the type of mindset and emotion of many members struggling with the end of an era.

Mary's club decided to rebrand, starting with a new logo design to include on members' T-shirts. When the new look was complete, all members received a shirt and were told to wear it at their next group meeting. A photographer would attend to capture the moment, and everyone dutifully showed up wearing their new attire as instructed, with the exception of a long-serving member named Susan. She steadfastly refused to wear the new T-shirt, and no amount of cajoling or peer pressure would get her to budge.

I was intrigued by the story, as well as Susan's rationale. As I probed deeper, Mary revealed the real reason for Susan's noncompliance. Several years prior, Susan's husband, Jerry, the founder of the club, had passed away. Susan felt that if she put on the T-shirt, her act would have represented a break from the past. The scenario was too painful, and Susan wasn't ready. Her counterparts did not share her experience. Even if a number of them understood her defiance (and may even have felt similarly), they did not speak up. Nor did they offer empathy. Susan's story was a raw, revealing glimpse into the psyche of the club leaders and members.

During the initial stages of organizational change, missteps frequently occur. In this case it was the organization's lack of recognition around the emotional impact that comes with change, as well as the need for empathy. When you transparently and authentically address the psychological stress of change, you increase the probability of buy-in to your change initiatives.

Solicit Feedback

Change management involves embarking on a journey, one that cannot occur in isolation. It is a process that requires feedback and meaningful dialogue, and allowing for disagreements and divergent opinions is healthy. Open discussions provide an opportunity for others to share opinions and alternatives, and Susan's story serves to illustrate this dual purpose on several levels.

First, it was a highly relevant example that others could relate to and learn from. Second, the organization was able to build on the learning and seek input across the board regarding larger scale change initiatives, such as introducing a variety of social media platforms to engage the existing membership and promote the benefits of belonging to a new cohort of potential members. The use of social media was previously sporadic, and not everyone was on board. The leaders and marketing department conducted surveys on the topic to take the pulse of the membership across the globe. They determined that members were open to increasing their knowledge while recognizing the benefits of attracting existing and new members to their events. Based on the feedback, the organization was able to take incremental steps to incorporate social media into their membership growth strategy. Existing members were encouraged to learn and become familiar with the tools, rather than being mandated to contribute.

Practice MMFI

MMFI means "make me feel important." Humans possess an intrinsic need to feel useful and valued. During change initiatives, it is essential for leaders to positively influence the process by encouraging their teams to participate. People will feel the need to change when *they* want to. Buy-in can't be forced, and your timetable for change may not gel with your team. However, if you have achieved credibility by building relationships and a positive reputation both internally and externally, it *is* possible to achieve momentum during the change process by validating the individual roles played by each member of your team.

In Susan's example, the area leader could have been more sensitive to her personal reasons for not wishing to wear the T-shirt. The leader could have engaged Susan in a conversation regarding her husband's history and legacy with the club. Perhaps they could have explored several options to find common ground, such as acknowledging his contribution or honoring his memory on the day of the new logo launch. Although Susan may still have chosen not to support the initiative, the fact remains that acknowledgment of Susan's feelings and past history was lacking. Making Susan feel that her feelings were important may have been the better alternative.

4. Prioritize Talent

An increasingly savvy, highly educated pool of talent is researching potential employers to learn more about the values of organizations and their leadership. Unfortunately, how employers recruit talent does not always yield optimum results, and that isn't necessarily due to the unsuitability of the candidates.

According to Peter Cappelli, George W. Taylor professor of management at the Wharton School and director of its Center for Human Resources, the hiring approach used by many companies today is often antiquated and problematic.[1] Cappelli notes that one-third of US organizations are failing to measure whether their hiring approach leads to good employees. They also waste energy by not developing a greater understanding of employee needs and *why* they leave a company, forgoing the chance to create a culture that provides opportunities that will make employees want to stay.

In addition, leaders are often unaware of how their current and future workforce view their managers and leaders and whether they believe they are receiving effective mentoring, motivation, and relationship-building. Often employee views are in stark opposition to the views of management and leadership, who believe that they are delivering on trust, transparency, and availability.

Adam Rogers, chief technology officer at Ultimate Software, has been quoted as saying, "We're witnessing a fundamental shift in how employees view their managers. Manager relationships aren't just about someone telling you how to do your job, it's a relationship that has a major impact on employee retention and happiness... Leaders should look at the ways they can leverage human resources and technology to get ahead of communication and trust breakdowns, and work closely with employees to redefine what it means to be a manager in the twenty-first century."[2]

It's one thing to meet the challenges associated with finding, hiring, and keeping great people. It's another to realize that achieving success in your quest directly relates to your current and future leadership skills. When you consider your own interview experiences and first few months in your previous jobs, what memories come to mind? You may not have known much about your employer simply because the information wasn't available. Perhaps your career began before the existence of headhunters, the proliferation of online recruitment platforms, or even the advent of the internet.

If you identify with any of those circumstances and you already possess a high level of awareness regarding how different the world is now, you may not be surprised by how differently your potential talent sees you and your leadership position, and what they expect their work experiences to be. By applying the following solutions, you, too, can drive your talent strategy to success.

Set a Gutsy Goal

As you reflect on your overarching company objective, think about its appeal. Is it bold enough to get the attention of your potential talent? Are you creating a mission with your workforce *as well as* your customers in mind?

Career seekers are intentional when choosing an employer. They have a myriad of options, and your big hairy goal needs to stand out from the crowd in order to attract them. Your future workforce wants you to be clear about why you are hiring them. They want to know how your organization is making a difference. The key question for you and your leadership team to be asking yourselves is: what is the higher purpose associated with my teams' daily activities?

The purpose needs to be framed in such a way that it appeals to their values. Andrew Scott (see Chapter 2) sums it up as follows: "We stress in the interview *why* they should come work for us. Our mission is to change a million lives per year by 2027. We thought, 'What's a crazy audacious goal that we can come up with?' We believe we are changing people's lives with the product that we serve. So we lead with that with everything we do. In every meeting we have, that's the first question. What is our mission? What are we working toward? Everything leads back to that mission."

Nurturing an employee-centric culture pays dividends. The concept involves an intentional effort to engage employees in the process of creating a great culture, one where they can relate to your organization's raison d'être and have their ideas heard and acted upon. In Andrew's business, the Pita Pit franchises, the focus is on healthy eating, and staff have bought into realizing their company's goal because they believe they are making a difference in the lives of their patrons through nutritious, affordable food. Scott and his team have not strayed from their mission. He continues to mentor them, support their development, and collaborate with them to keep and build their base of loyal clientele.

Manage Talent to Stay Competitive

Your talent's expectations still matter greatly. They need evidence of a clear opportunity path, access to mentors, education to further career development, and recognition regarding the importance of work/life balance. Your task as a leader is to harness a willingness and emotional stamina to continually redesign, rebuild, and recalibrate your talent management strategy. As your organization emerges from this or any period of acute disruption, it will be your talent that continues to give your organization the competitive advantage. Your talent management strategy is one factor that you *can* control in any circumstance. Creating outstanding products and services cannot happen without implementing a *people first* philosophy, as you will see in subsequent chapters.

REFINING YOUR leadership skills requires self-motivation and determination because we have entered an era where the demands on leaders have never been greater. The stakes have never been higher and the workforce is more conscious of the world. People have no qualms expressing their desire to contribute in a meaningful way. As a leader, people expect you to express your humanity as well as be up to the task of leading.

Balancing these demands against the backdrop of uncertainty and unrelenting change may feel daunting at times. However, trusting in yourself, your abilities, your supporters, and the talent that surrounds you can result in highly gratifying experiences, especially when you choose a growth mindset over a fixed one (p. 14).

Real-Time Takeaways

- Take the time to honestly appraise your motives in your journey to leadership and the choice to remain in the role. Are you inspired and ready to provide real-time leadership?

- Outstanding interpersonal communication skills are not a passing fad. Be mindful of how others perceive your intentions and strive for transparency.

- Real-time leaders advocate collaboration and inclusiveness. The best ideas aren't necessarily your own.

- Encouraging accountability is a strength. People want to take pride and ownership of their work and respond positively when given the opportunity.

- Look for the good in change, whether it occurs unexpectedly or intentionally. Recognize that individual responses will vary. Resistance is instinctive and empathy goes a long way in circumstances of change.

- Re-skilling your workforce and ensuring your talent supply is plentiful remain critical. Relegating your talent strategy to an afterthought can harm your organization's future readiness.

Real-Time Action Step

Choose the essential real-time leadership skill that resonates with you the most. It may change over the course of your career and time. What could you do to ensure that you remain ready and relevant when applying this one particular skill, right now?

THE HUMAN FACTOR

"He has the personality of a dial tone."

PHYLLIS DILLER

ENTER BILL, a leader you can't forget... for all the wrong reasons.

Bill, the senior departmental head, delivered his annual update clinically and barely managed a glance at his team during this entire speech. The news was shocking and a huge blow. As Bill imposed a new reality of employment uncertainty on his team, people were squirming in their seats. Looking around the room, I could see the blood draining from the faces in the crowd. Some people began to cry. Others were mumbling under their breath. It was painful to witness a leader who was so completely out of touch with the impact of his words. I am certain that many would have loved to run for the exit but couldn't escape. To make matters worse, Bill, aka the "bearer of bad news," singled out specific individuals by name:

unwilling supervisors who were being nominated for clean-up duty. Simply put, Bill delegated the task of providing care and compassion for his employees to his managers.

As he walked off the stage, my thoughts were jumbled and I struggled to compose myself with only minutes before it was my turn to rally the troops and deliver my "Change Starts with You" presentation. The timing was awful, unexpected, cruel. No one had informed me that I would have to follow bad news Bill. This was because the meeting planner also had no idea that the department head would choose that precise moment to destroy his team's hope for their future. In an instant, this upbeat group who were looking forward to an afternoon of fun and learning completely switched off. To say that the air was sucked out of the room was an understatement. And unfortunately, Bill was completely out of touch with his team's reaction to his speech.

The words of Development Dimensions International's senior vice president, Richard S. Wellins, PhD, are apropos where this story is concerned: "Far more leadership failures are attributed to insensitivity rather than stupidity."[1] Had Bill invested in himself by polishing his empathy skills and prioritizing the building of relationships with his employees, the impact of his pronouncement may have been received differently.

CAST YOUR mind back to your first job... What memories do you have of your immediate manager or supervisor? Did they spend time getting to know you? Were they supportive? Did they provide you with sufficient training? Was the purpose of each task explained in such a way that you understood the connection between your role and its importance to your organization's mission? Was your workplace a fun place to be?

In 1849, French writer Jean-Baptiste Alphonse Karr wrote "plus ça change, plus c'est la même chose," which means the more things change, the more they stay the same. His words remain relevant when you consider what truly makes the world of business revolve. It's the personalities, the memorable encounters, the real-life experiences that are etched in our memories and shared in boardrooms, blog posts, and business lunches. It's the professional relationships that enrich our careers and leadership experiences, often becoming the subject matter of books like this.

Business still requires human interaction, and a leader needs the ability to genuinely connect and relate to their workforce. No matter how good your knowledge and skill sets, you cannot ignore that business is about the people first. The degree to which a leader makes a powerful, personal, and lasting positive impression is in direct proportion to the quality of their employee relationships.

People First

I have yet to meet a successful leader who isn't pulled in a million directions simultaneously. Leaders like the CEO of MakerKids, Jennifer Turliuk, whom you will meet in the next chapter, are acutely aware that they could not have achieved their vision without having a great team supporting and leading key initiatives. What makes these leaders stand out is that they recognize what it means to put people first. Without prioritizing the human side of business, they realize that it will be difficult, if not impossible, for their organizations to grow, remain relevant, continue to evolve, and meet the demands of customers.

In a recent article[2] focusing on the importance of people in the age of transformation, the authors note "that the main implication is that when leaders think about investing in technology, they should first think about investing in the *people* who can make that technology useful." This ought to be a high priority for all types of organizations. Such was the case in September 2016, when the largest tech merger in history took place. Dell, MSD Partners, and Silver Lake completed the process of acquiring EMC Corporation for $67 billion. Dell Technologies subsequently became the world's largest privately controlled tech company.

Earlier that year EMC World hosted its annual event in Las Vegas with sixteen thousand attendees from their Fortune 5,000 client base. The news of the merger was already public knowledge, although at that time EMC shareholders had not yet voted to accept the deal. Michael Dell, chairman and CEO of Dell, joined EMC chairman and CEO Joe Tucci onstage after Tucci gave his last keynote address as the head of EMC. Tucci concluded with the following words: "I can tell you right now, this is not the end of something great . . . This is the beginning of something greater."

At the conclusion of the event, I had the honor of leading a special session with EMC's global senior sales engineering leaders on the topic of retaining top talent. It was critically important to this client to provide the attendees with tools to help them lead proactively and keep their best people engaged, motivated, and positive during periods of transition.

There was something uniquely special about the team that these sales engineering leaders managed. As technologists, these sales engineers possessed outstanding relational skills as well as the tech skills to resolve a client's problem and provide the right support. They represented a highly sought-after talent pool because they could work with their clients on complex technology and carry out conversations at a human level.

Following the successful merger of Dell and EMC, talent management remains top of mind for the newly named enterprise, Dell Technologies. Equally important is the priority placed on building and sustaining enduring customer relationships. Real-time leaders are developing brands that are both employee- and customer-centric, recognizing that a great customer experience is dependent upon creating a great employee experience first.

As leaders, you understand how you profoundly influence every aspect of your organization. Finding the secret sauce to successfully lead a mix of personalities need not be elusive. The possibilities turn into probabilities the more you are able to sharpen your self-awareness and remain a lifelong learner. As Indra Nooyi, former CEO of PepsiCo, wisely said, "Just because you are CEO, don't think you have landed."

Ultimately, your teams, employees, and primary stakeholders see you as the key individual providing the overall direction and presiding over critical business decisions. Your imprint is felt throughout all levels of your enterprise, evidenced by your mission, values, culture, and talent pool. Some of you may wield your influence overtly, while others are quietly impacting strategy, hiring processes, and customer-centric initiatives. In the long run, no matter how high tech your organization may become, the culmination of all your efforts and decisions for which you are responsible will continue to touch the lives of many.

However, the burning question is how do real-time leaders put people first in the midst of all the changes to the workforce discussed in Chapter 2? The answer lies in a leader's willingness to meet current and future talent pools where they are.

A great customer
experience is
dependent
upon creating
a great employee
experience first.

———

When you come to terms with the reality that many members of the emerging workforce may choose to go down a different career path, either as independent contractors or remote workers, you can adapt accordingly.

From your employee's vantage point, the single most important aspect of effective leadership is making yourself available for your team, regardless of whether they work remotely or in the same physical location. This necessitates time management on your part. Are you accessible in person, by phone, or through whatever means necessary to connect in a meaningful manner? Planning and organizing your schedule to regularly make time for a conversation is not simply a task to check off your to-do list. It should be a leadership priority.

Do you possess the essential skills to lead in real time *and* manage your organization in a future-thinking way? Successful leaders are cognizant of their responsibilities and are mindful of organizing their priorities. Although accomplishing the routine aspects of work is still important, leaders cannot lose sight of the need to get the right things done. And *the right things* means prioritizing people as well as projects. When you find yourself getting caught up in the minutiae, realize that you are putting your ability to perform at the optimal level at risk. Having numerous balls in the air may come with the territory. However, each time you choose to prioritize less important tasks over your team's needs, you compromise your ability to be effective.

Leaders often lament the fact that they find themselves being pulled in many different directions. With so many demands on a leader's time, deciphering levels of urgency among important issues and tasks can be problematic. At the same time, leaders who are personally in step with their team members have a greater opportunity to strengthen the relationship and harness their respective intrinsic motivation levels. Make it a priority to study the practices of leaders whose displays of humanness and humility have yielded loyalty and commitment among employees.

The Pirate Life

"It's better to be a pirate than to join the navy."

When Apple cofounder Steve Jobs used this phrase with his team of developers who were working on the Macintosh in 1983, his intent was to motivate and inspire, to captivate his team's imagination as they carved out their own identity and innovative creations. It worked. The symbolism of his expression subsequently became legendary, as the team created their own pirate flag,[3] with the Apple logo embedded in the skull-and-crossbones design. The flag flew proudly atop their retreat location in Carmel, hoisted again at the company's Cupertino headquarters on its fortieth anniversary.

Jobs's famous quotation resonates with me for several reasons. First, it depicts the state of many employees today who want to fly solo, unburdened by bosses who micromanage and policies that they consider restrictive. As workplaces continue to undergo radical transformation, the most effective leaders are recognizing that their organizations benefit exponentially when divergent ideas are encouraged rather than stifled. Second, Jobs's words to his Macintosh team remind me of my first boss, as I started my career in the same year, several months later.

After finishing university, my first job was in the advertising sales department at a radio station in Sydney. When I arrived, I was shown to my sparsely furnished desk, atop which sat a lone telephone, some empty files, and a few sundry stationery supplies. There were no computers for the sales team, although a number of managers had either large mainframe computers or the early versions of IBM office computers. A noisy telex machine sat in the corner of the office, spewing out endless reams of paper at the beginning and end of each workday.

I had no interest in nor any familiarity with electronics, save the photocopy machine. Nor did I have any awareness about Steve Jobs and the technology revolution taking place at the Macintosh office half a world away. I had no inkling about what it meant to be a nonconformist, as our workplace was almost completely devoid of troublemakers or rule breakers, with the exception of my colleague Daniel, who stirred the pot and delighted in spreading gossip at every opportunity.

If I had known how to be a contrarian or a pirate like Steve Jobs's team at Macintosh, I would have rebelled against my sales manager and likely been fired for causing a mutiny. Sadly, I was indeed one of the seaman apprentices in our "navy," and Veronica, my immediate boss, was my hapless, scatterbrained captain, who had a lovely corner office with a multimillion-dollar view of the harbor. Veronica was the only person among 120 staff who would often forget to go to the payroll office to collect her pay packets. Janice, the paymistress (yes, that was her title), would call to remind Veronica that her piles of cash (yes, we were paid in cash) were accumulating and it might be a good idea if she walked over to collect them. As I was situated right outside Veronica's office, I would often hear her shrieks of laughter every time Janice called.

Bob, Veronica's chain-smoking superior, was based in Melbourne. As one of the rear admirals, he would occasionally surface on the upper deck, taking over Veronica's office whenever he pleased.

It was Bob who first interviewed me for the sales assistant position. I had been thrilled to receive his telephone call informing me that I had been shortlisted for the job after having sent over a hundred letters and copies of my resume to every newspaper, radio, and television station in my home state. I had completed university with an honors degree in political science with aspirations of becoming a foreign correspondent, yet it was almost impossible to find work in the midst of a deep recession.

I was unemployed for almost a year after finishing my degree, securing occasional work in my father's retail store during that time. When Bob called, I felt relief and excitement. I saw the opportunity in the sales department as a door-opener to a position in the news department. Although my aspirations to become a traveling journalist never materialized, my career in advertising turned out to be an exciting adventure that lasted a decade. Unfortunately, during the early years with Veronica, I often felt lost at sea.

Our department was responsible for the advertising sales of twenty regional radio stations across the country as part of a network of rural and national stations. My position involved liaising with clients and station management, learning the ropes of selling airtime while assisting my boss in an administrative capacity. Our office was located within the Sydney radio operations of one of our flagship stations, and my sales colleagues who represented the national group were located on the same floor. I learned quickly that the network's number-one priority was revenue generation. The floor was always a flurry of activity as the sales department staff were often making calls, coming or going from client appointments, kibitzing with colleagues, or celebrating success following the results of quarterly ratings surveys. It was a very fun atmosphere, and there were many moments when work didn't feel like work.

Except during my interactions with Veronica.

On one specific occasion, Veronica began sharing some internal information with me and abruptly stopped herself.

She ended the conversation with the following words: "I don't need to tell you anything that is happening around here." Fast forward almost forty years, and I can remember this interlude as if it happened yesterday. It wasn't unusual for Veronica to blow hot and cold. She would often vocalize her own self-doubt, and I discovered later that she had never been in a leadership position. Her role marked a return to the workforce after a significant period of time off. As I was also new to the game, it was difficult to grasp the key aspects of my role since Veronica herself wasn't entirely sure what to do. Not a great combination for confidence-building or engagement. When the stress became too much, I frequently felt the burden of her attempts to manage the challenge. Veronica stayed with the company for only three months. Her sudden departure meant that I needed to navigate the nuances on my own, until Bob found a replacement.

I share this story for several reasons. First, the fact that I can recall the entire cast of characters in detail indicates that the memories are still fresh, even after a significant period of time has passed. Second, I remember the put-downs and lack of transparency. There was no opportunity to talk about my aspirations or the meaning of what we were doing in the grand scheme of things. Third, it was surprising to me that Veronica left after only three months. Leadership turnover is certainly a sign of instability and doesn't go unnoticed.

Bad Bosses Are Expensive

To say that no one likes to be bossed around is an understatement. A bossy boss is the worst example of a leader, yet it seems that many bosses simply cannot help themselves, even if they know better. Even worse, bad bosses cost companies a fortune.[4]

And although bad bosses are as old as Methuselah, the problem persists. Here we are in the knowledge economy, the age of unparalleled digital transformation, yet some of the most highly educated people at the helm of many organizations still don't get it. That's because intelligence and self-awareness are traits that do not always come hand in hand. Some leaders possess both, but others will never grasp the significance of acquiring the latter. The more that leaders exert control over their workforce, regardless of their rank, the more turned off people become.

Although it is possible that people can choose to transform themselves, all too often bad bosses have caused so much damage that organizations may find themselves either soul searching to deal with the aftermath or having to start from scratch to rebuild their cultures. The reality is that no enterprise can be successful without great leadership *and* great talent. Today's talent is bold, savvy, expressive, and more educated than that of any other period in history. And their threshold for tolerating poor leadership is low. When leaders fully embrace this concept, they can make better choices about who they appoint to management positions while becoming more cognizant of their value to the overall functioning of their organizations.

Disruption and uncertainty have become the norm. Despite the chaos and frenzied pace of change, one constant remains: leaders need to set the example. When they do not, the fallout is costly. And depending on the stability of an enterprise, recovery may take years. In today's environment where a leader's reputation is synonymous with that of their organization, being in a perpetual state of damage control brought about by lousy leadership makes no sense. Yet many leaders aren't getting the memo.

REAL-TIME LEADERS are constantly focused on the people side of business, recognizing that the strengths or weaknesses in boss/employee relationships have a significant impact on the bottom line. There is a high cost to poor leadership choices. Especially when rolling the dice on leaders who are unprepared or who are incapable of immediately assessing real-time situations, including ongoing volatility, pressure from key stakeholders, and shifts in employee expectations.

I learned firsthand that an employee's experiences of leaders and employers leave a lasting impression. What has become even more apparent today with the rise of social media is that virtually every move that an organization makes is under the microscope, which is why it is more important than ever to have the right leadership in the right place but also to develop that leadership continually.

Real-Time Takeaways

- The degree to which a leader makes a powerful, personal, and lasting positive impression is in direct proportion to the quality of their employee relationships. Whether you are a seasoned leader or a new one, your influence is likely to be felt and remembered.

- Teams relish the opportunity to create their own identity while discovering their creativity. Let them flourish and raise their own flag.

- The *most* important aspect of effective leadership is making yourself available for your team, regardless of whether they work remotely or in the same physical location.

➤ The high price of low morale can be traced back to ineffective and out-of-touch leadership. You can dramatically improve the workplace atmosphere by removing leaders who are either out of their depth or otherwise unsuitable for the position.

Real-Time Action Step

The simple act of genuinely connecting with a team member either remotely or in person, even to simply "shoot the breeze," goes a long way. Make it a habit to intentionally take an interest and create a two-way dialogue with one employee each working day.

LEADERSHIP STRATEGY IS BUSINESS STRATEGY

"To add value to others, one must first value others."
JOHN C. MAXWELL

JENNIFER TURLIUK is the CEO and founder of MakerKids franchise, the world's largest makerspace helping children learn STEM (science, technology, engineering, math) through an array of after-school and online educational programs on coding, robotics, and Minecraft. Her fascinating entrepreneurial success story is remarkable on many levels.

At the age of twelve, Jennifer coded and created her own website for a book project on *Harry Potter*. Her website went viral and was featured in a major children's magazine. The experience inspired her to pursue her passion for technology and helping children develop STEM skills.

Today, not only is Jennifer a role model for children and young adults, but she also has specific insights and business practices that are cementing her as a leader in her industry. But, ultimately, Jennifer is a leader who understands deeply that she is responsible for acquiring self-knowledge and mindfulness to lead herself before leading others.

When I asked Jennifer what she thinks leaders need to do to lead successfully, she replied that they need to let "employees be the CEOs of their own positions and to empower them, to give them flexibility, match their interests, passions, and goals with positions available." Her approach is to give "people the opportunity to be creative and feel like they have ownership of the company." Jennifer explained that she "treats the company like a third-party entity that we all report to... that it's not synonymous with me (even though I own it). It enables [employees] to feel more responsibility and productivity toward it."

Whether you are a CEO, entrepreneur, or executive team leader, your leadership responsibilities must evolve along with your workforce. Command and control leadership styles are being called into question, and employee values and expectations are not necessarily the same as yours. Real-time leaders will need to find ways to transform themselves, their own leaders, as well as their organizations against a backdrop of transformation. Many of you, as well as the leaders you choose to lead in your organizations, will need to lead differently. Some of you may even need to get back to the basics (see Chapter 3) if you are going to effectively connect with your teams.

FOR YEARS, I have been a fan of Jim Clifton, chairman and CEO of Gallup. His company has surveyed millions of employees and leaders across the globe for the past forty years. Time and again, Gallup's research confirms that companies in an array of industries put the wrong leaders into the wrong job over 80 percent of the time! If this alarming statistic doesn't get your attention, I am not sure what it will take to get you and your organization to act—and act fast.

With so much out of your control, the one area you can control is who you decide to place into this esteemed and influential position of leading others. You can take positive action to recalibrate when you know it's the right thing to do. Bad bosses directly contribute to high levels of disengagement (see Chapter 4).

But what is even more alarming is that Gallup's findings confirm that 65 percent of managers are not engaged or are actively disengaged.[1] That's not the workforce. That's the leadership.

Please take a moment to let that sink in.

During my ten-year tenure at the radio network, I encountered several leaders whose myopic views, antiquated approaches, and shocking behaviors made a lasting impression for all the wrong reasons. One example was Felix, a misogynist who once told me that I would "never make it as a manager." He was renowned for his temper and discriminatory attitudes toward his female staff in particular. I am still incredulous when I think about how often Felix would dismiss the opinions of women in leadership who were lower on the pecking order and prevent them from expressing themselves during meetings or informal business discussions. Since then I've come across many people who are disillusioned in their careers following similar negative encounters with their bosses, and that says a lot about the current state of leadership.

In the digital economy, employees are hungry to advance their skills and make progress. In a report by the Institute for the Future and Dell Technologies, findings indicate that 85 percent of jobs that will exist in 2030 haven't been invented yet.[2] They predict that "instead of people chasing jobs, work will chase people... that (we need to) get ready for a lifetime of skills training and retraining in real time." In this context, it is

Realizing organizational goals cannot happen without first determining the type of leaders your enterprise requires.

━━━━━━━

alarming to note that disengagement levels continue to escalate and employee retention will be significantly compromised. And according to go2HR,[3] over 40 percent of employees will leave their positions within a year if they do not receive essential training to effectively perform in their work. The race is on to ensure that organizations are providing optimal opportunities for developing their people through training programs, especially when they are reconfiguring workplaces to incorporate new technologies such as AI, machine learning, or blockchain. But people development isn't only about teams. It's also about leaders. To create and sustain success in the digitized economy, real-time leaders must take action and confront hard truths regarding their attitudes and antiquated approaches.

What is your organization's leaders doing to develop *their* skills and address their future readiness?

Develop Leaders as well as the Workforce

Defining the direction of your business is at the core of all successful enterprises. However, is your direction giving equal attention to the leadership attributes that breathe life into your strategy?

Are your leaders prepared to drive change?

Are they able to create a compelling employee-centric brand that draws in talent?

Leadership strategy precedes business strategy. Realizing organizational goals cannot happen without first determining the type of leaders your enterprise requires. In the absence of leadership willingness to make the difficult decisions, to create essential change, and to inspire teams to collaborate, your business strategy stalls.[4]

Leading organizations recognize that their current and emerging workforce crave learning opportunities and greater connection to the purpose of their work. But leaders also need professional development to break down their own internal resistance and barriers to change. Top-notch organizations are in tune with workforce trends and the imperative to align business strategy with leadership strategy. They are constantly recalibrating educational methodologies to train leaders and are willing to create opportunities for leaders to learn to lead differently.

When was the last time your organization rigorously assessed the effectiveness of your leadership development programs?

Unfortunately, some organizations are reactionary when it comes to creating effective leadership development programs. Behavioral or skill deficiencies in leaders may rise to the surface, taking on a sense of urgency, yet the delivery methods to help leaders address the gaps are undeveloped or entirely absent. A sudden need to get a leader up to speed has the potential to create unintended consequences. For example, an organization may end up scrambling to alter work schedules and reprioritize projects, which may lead to increased stress and pressure for all. The sad reality is that too many leaders aren't prepared or willing to lead themselves, their teams, and their organizations.

Donald Cooper is a professional colleague and friend who is a real-time leader, as was his father. Donald's father, Jack Cooper, together with an incredible team, built Cooper Canada Ltd. into one of the world's leading makers of protective sports equipment and fine leather goods, most famous for its hockey equipment and baseball gloves. Donald has a great phrase for describing leaders who are in denial of the truth: "The beginning of wisdom is the recognition of reality."

Donald's philosophy aptly reflects the state of current circumstances. Leaders are failing to address significant gaps regarding change management, gender equality, developing talent, digitizing their businesses, undertaking ongoing succession planning, and improving their emotional intelligence quotient. Each one of these imperatives needs attention, otherwise they will drive disengagement and disenchantment in the workforce. A leader's individual biases and outdated perspectives do contribute to an employee's decision to stay at or leave an organization. And high staff turnover may result in challenges such as a reinforcement of the status quo, low morale, and a detrimental impact on the bottom line.

What follows are the three actions that any leader or organization should take to ensure they have engaged real-time leaders who can lead effectively through transformation into the future.

1. Prioritize Change Management Education

Change management remains a preoccupation for many CEOs. Among the many "what keeps CEOs up at night" surveys, one fascinating read is the PricewaterhouseCoopers research document called "The Anxious Optimist in the Corner Office."[5] This paper describes top leadership concerns across the globe. Although there were some variances in responses and rankings, there were many common denominators amongst leaders' concerns, including geopolitical instability, talent management, and economic uncertainty. Chief among the CEOs' worries is the speed of technological change and the need to take advantage of new technologies.

Similar studies have also confirmed that digital transformation including AI, machine learning, and blockchain technologies remain top priorities in the C-suite. Leaders are also conscious of the need to leverage the right talent to meet the challenge, while mitigating job losses resulting from increased digitization. No surprise then that many leaders are obsessed with the dramatically shifting landscape and are anxious about the implications for the future. But to make matters complicated, the 2019 Lee Hecht Harrison research transformation report[6] revealed that 85 percent of participants say people in their organizations don't have the leadership skills they need to drive transformation.

Peter, a client of mine in the financial services sector, is a real-time leader who recognized this very issue was preventing transformation in his own company.

Peter's business is undergoing explosive growth, but he recognizes that growth also brings challenge. He identified a need for critical technology to serve clients more efficiently and, ultimately, to move his organization forward during expansion. As the CEO of his firm, he encountered strong resistance from his leadership team regarding implementing these new methodologies. Peter quickly discovered that there were deeper reasons behind his team's reluctance to participate in the learning initiative. To meet internal and external demands, Peter's leaders needed to gain a fundamental understanding of technology gaps and hire the right people with the skill sets to address them. But his team felt uncomfortable with the concept of acquiring essential new skills themselves to make this happen.

Peter candidly shared with me that the situation served as an opportunity to reevaluate the entire spectrum of his organization's learning programs, to address internal challenges, and to prioritize leadership development initiatives and hiring practices. His greatest realization was the need to address the subculture of "change aversion" that prevailed among senior leaders. If the leaders at the top were not buying in, a trickle-down effect would ensue. Their resistance would be reflected in their attitudes and actions toward their teams, leading to doubt, disengagement, and higher levels of dissatisfaction across the board.

If you want your workforce to adapt and embrace change, the first step is to ensure that your senior leaders are in step with and able to drive change initiatives. Without modeling the behavior you desire for your team (i.e., to *be* an agent of change), achieving buy-in is much more difficult.

2. Zero In on Gender Bias and Discrimination

My example of the discriminatory Felix (p. 95) still lives on in today's workplaces unfortunately. Despite global legislation mandating greater levels of female representation on company boards, progress has been sluggish in equal pay, opportunities for promotion, and positive perceptions of women as capable and effective leaders. Although studies confirm that there has been a decline in "experiences that drive many women out of their careers"[7] (blatant sexual harassment and assault), there was an increase in hostility toward women (gender harassment) from 76 percent in 2016 to 92 percent in 2018. The #MeToo movement has further highlighted the problem of ongoing sexual harassment and assault in numerous industries (with both men and women as victims).

For more than thirty years, McKinsey Global Institute has led the way in researching the correlation between improved team performance, communication, productivity, and profitability when women are at the helm. In one of the most extensive global studies carried out on the importance of advancing women's equality,[8] McKinsey described a scenario in which eradicating gender discrimination would add $28 trillion (26 percent) to the value of the global economy by 2025.

However, despite the mountain of evidence from reputable organizations like McKinsey that demonstrates the return on investment of promoting women to leadership positions, many companies remain in a time warp, continuing to pay lip service to equality and gender diversity. How does one explain that leaders who profess to understand the business case for women still remain intransigent? The answer is clear: gender bias that remains engrained in organizational structures cannot be eradicated until there is a total commitment to shift mindsets. And this shift has to start at the top.

My recent encounters with clients who are making inroads to alter gender imbalance in their organizations caused me to reflect on others who haven't been as successful. One senior vice president told me that when he shared news regarding the promotion of one of his managers prior to her taking maternity leave, several male managers questioned the timing and even had difficulty accepting that she had earned the promotion. In another situation, a major retailer received feedback from both men and women in leadership positions expressing their concerns about their company's "women in leadership" initiative. Several female leaders said they were uncomfortable being singled out, while several men felt it was unfair that they were excluded from participating.

Without first isolating the root causes of persistent gender inequality and, second, educating leadership at all levels, the consequences of inaction will become evident in terms of talent attrition. An OmniPulse survey commissioned by Randstad revealed that 80 percent of women agree that they would switch employers if they felt another company had greater gender equality. In a company press release[9] following the survey, Audra Jenkins, chief diversity and inclusion officer for Randstad North America, said that for "companies that fail to establish an inclusive workplace, attracting and retaining quality talent will be a major challenge in the years ahead."

To suggest that all leaders are unaware of the business consequences would be inaccurate. However, despite the best intentions of those who are addressing biases head-on, workplace departures over these issues persist, leaving organizations exposed to potential negative consequences to their bottom line and to their corporate image. Unfortunately, there are similar scenarios playing out daily in industries worldwide. When leaders take meaningful action to address biases, it is more likely that a positive trickle-down effect will be felt.

3. Provide Feedback Training

"Catch them doing it right" was Ken Blanchard's evergreen advice to leaders in his One Minute Manager book series. His philosophy rings true today with an even deeper meaning.

How leaders manage themselves in any communication is 100 percent within their control. In terms of providing on-the-job feedback, the difference for the recipient and the organization can be immeasurable when it's done well and potentially disastrous when it is not. The unfortunate reality is that employees continue to be turned off by negative feedback regarding their overall performance, let alone discussions regarding their future with their employer. A Gallup survey[10] revealed that four out of five employees actively seek new opportunities following their annual performance review, and only 14.5 percent of managers say that they are effective when providing either positive or negative feedback. These numbers indicate that there is huge potential for improvement.

Think about the implications of a manager's inadequate communications with their employees about career development and performance. What message does that send to an employee about how their value is perceived both now and in the future? When it is clear that an individual has high potential and is an asset to your organization, there can be significant mutual benefit if they are given the right direction and support.

More food for thought: an EY Global survey on employee trust[11] notes that some of the top influencing factors across all age groups are the degree of open and transparent communication, frequency of two-way dialogue, feedback, and willingness to hear their point of view. The millennial generation is now officially the largest[12] adult population in the US. But their expectations regarding feedback and professional development are significantly different[13] from the generational cohorts preceding them (p. 30). They want and expect weekly feedback and place a high priority on opportunities for professional development.

Throughout the years, leaders have shared with me examples of poor delivery of feedback that they have either personally received or heard about in their workplace. One such example that made a deep impression on me came from Deborah, a senior marketing manager for a renowned home care services organization. Over the period of a year, Deborah witnessed growing discontent among the core leadership team, a dedicated group that pioneered significant initiatives to innovate and grow the business.

During one management meeting, frustrations reached a crescendo when the VP of HR reported on the findings of the previous month's exit interviews. Resignations included four support care coordinators, the director of client services, a director of nursing, an accounts receivable manager, and two

Hiring and developing
your managers
goes hand in hand
with your talent
management strategy.

physiotherapists. The comments from these exit interviews about how several leaders provided feedback, both formal and informal, generated a heated discussion. What was made clear is that those employees who left the organization had slowly lost confidence in their leader, as well as themselves, and reached a point where remaining in their positions was no longer tenable.

The dynamic between a leader and an employee (who may also be a leader) at any level can be the difference in that individual's decision to stay at or leave an organization. Your workforce needs to know that you are helping them to develop their strengths by investing in their careers. Performance reviews work best when they are less formal. It need not happen through a specific structure or format and is often more impactful when it occurs in real time. What matters more is your effort to genuinely connect and provide regular feedback.

IF YOUR leaders are not trained to be successful in the above three competencies, the impact will ricochet throughout your organization. Talented employees are constantly evaluating employment options and are heavily influenced by the relationship with their immediate manager. To mitigate the possibility of losing good employees, ask these questions of your leaders:

- Do they understand the needs of their workforce and the values shift that is occurring culturally and demographically?

- Are their mindsets fixed or open?

- Are they exceptional listeners and collaborators?

Your answers may illuminate some harsh truths regarding the status of your leaders' collective readiness to embrace a different paradigm. When team members have expressed concerns about a manager at any level, ignoring the issue or hoping that their worries will dissipate is a major mistake. A lack of action can further exacerbate low engagement among employees.

Hiring and developing your managers goes hand in hand with your talent management strategy. Your goal is to ensure that you are investing wisely with your time, your energy, and everything associated with creating the best leaders possible.

Real-Time Takeaways

- Evaluating leadership performance is just as important as the attention and energy given to assessing employee performance.

- Prioritizing your leadership strategy is a precursor to your business strategies. Without ensuring that the right leaders are in the right place at the right time, planning a company's future direction will be more arduous.

- Real-time leaders ensure that they are up to speed with their own professional development, specifically in the areas of change management, unconscious bias, and effective communication, particularly where feedback is concerned.

- Eliminating antiquated attitudes and approaches to leadership will benefit the entire spectrum of your organization.

- Great leaders view their employee relationships as opportunities for stronger partnerships. They possess a willingness and openness to learn from any team member, any time.

Real-Time Action Step

Review this chapter to illuminate the potential for improving your leadership teams' professional development. Identify one area of focus, whether that is eradicating gender bias or amping up your training on how to deliver feedback, and commit to taking action over the next thirty days.

ENGAGEMENT IS EVERGREEN

"When people are financially invested, they want a return. When people are emotionally invested, they want to contribute."
SIMON SINEK

SEVERAL YEARS ago, I had the pleasure of meeting Philip and his wife, Ann, at a local networking event. They were founders of several highly successful start-ups and were excitedly embarking on a new venture. Philip and Ann invited me to view their office space, a twenty-thousand-square-foot space located in Gastown, a trendy heritage zone in downtown Vancouver. I began working with them, helping with their hiring strategies to bring in leaders, supervisors, and frontline technology specialists. It was an exciting project, and many details were carefully executed. The owners recognized that there was indeed a strong market for their cloud-based suite of offerings and correctly predicted that the demand for their services would escalate. Although explosive growth arrived more quickly than anticipated, these business leaders were ready for the challenge.

In order to be successful, their supervisors and workforce needed to be well versed in the technology. Although Philip and Ann did not have the depth of their employees' expertise, they recognized that being accessible and available was paramount. Creating the ideal work environment where everyone enjoyed camaraderie and fun was also top of mind.

In the early days of their respective careers, Philip and Ann had witnessed firsthand both outstanding as well as poor examples of implementing such initiatives. If they were going to keep new talent engaged, they needed to follow a specific trajectory. So, from the moment a new hire walked through the doors, Philip and Ann anticipated their immediate need to feel part of the business. They both understood that the first stages of building their business required a carefully designed program to educate and engage employees while creating a dynamic experience.

Engage to Win

If you perform a quick Google search using the keywords *employee engagement*, it yields millions and millions of results—at least it did for me at the time of writing of this book. The importance of this subject has not diminished since it was first introduced in a psychology paper written in 1990 by Professor William Kahn of Boston University. Kahn describes employee engagement as a state of commitment to a particular role in the workplace, "an identity and a relationship that offers fulfillment."[1]

Keeping your workforce happy and engaged need not be complicated, so long as proactive solutions are in place and aren't neglected over the long haul. But providing tangible motivators such as great pay and benefit packages aren't always the answer.

Survey after survey links job dissatisfaction primarily to the manager/employee relationship,[2] resulting in billions of lost productivity dollars. Gallup notes that this recent significant drop in employee engagement is anomalistic, given that past trends showed improvement. The survey cites a number of factors that may have contributed to the decline. Specifically, the societal unrest following the killing of George Floyd by persons in authority positions, an overall sense of geopolitical uncertainty, and leaders' unclear communication during the pandemic.

Unfortunately, employee disengagement can be a vicious cycle when problems are left unresolved, and the consequences are challenging to dislodge. Here's what can happen when your employees are disengaged.

Distrust and Dysfunction

Recently, several senior managers in the public sector shared with me their resentment regarding the top echelons of their leadership. The managers described their C-suite as an inept, self-serving group who, for the most part, were buying time until retirement. The office politics and dysfunction was rampant, yet no one was prepared to take action. As I listened to the managers describe their plight, I asked them to consider what it would be like if they were to reveal their innermost concerns and meet with their C-suite leaders? They expressed feeling trapped and fearful that if they addressed their leaders directly, they would risk losing their jobs. They had lost faith in their leadership and were left feeling uninspired, without hope, and lacking the desire to look for solutions.

As the discussion progressed, it was clear that the growing distrust was the core issue at every level of their organization. Since the C-suite appeared to have checked out, their managers were also switching off. In turn, employees were increasingly frustrated and disinterested as the toxicity escalated and spread throughout their organization. When the bonds of trust are broken and irreparable, the consequences can be dire. First, there is a pervasive sense of hopelessness and lack of positive momentum, which then leads to a decline in productivity and morale. Next, an organization risks losing valuable employees as well as customers. And, of course, all of this leads to a detrimental impact on the bottom line.

Breaching the Psychological Contract

Hearing the story of the checked-out C-suite from those senior managers reminded me of one of my own leadership experiences. Although my boss Phyllis had not lost interest in her job and was far from biding her time waiting for retirement, the glowing picture she painted in my job interview of the training I would receive and the open-door policy that she preached to all staff bore no resemblance to reality. After a few short weeks, my initial excitement fizzled. There was nothing pleasant about my working relationship with Phyllis because, I soon realized, it was up to me to sink or swim. Phyllis's negatively focused performance reviews, her reneging on details of my compensation package, and her total impatience in helping me learn the ropes only hastened my disenchantment.

I remember Phyllis losing her temper as I tried to grasp the basics of our software program. We sat side by side at the computer in my office as she had a total meltdown. As I watched her turn a bright shade of purple with rage, I couldn't help but notice that her face matched her outfit. I tried to hide my fear as the tears welled in my eyes. It was a pivotal moment.

When I worked with Phyllis, I was unfamiliar with the term *psychological contract*. This expression pertains to the unspoken relationship between an employer and employee. Unlike an employment contract, the psychological contract is informal and intangible, yet it sets the tone of the dynamic between both parties. At the time, I had little knowledge of this expression or other leadership business terminology. Nonetheless, I discovered quickly what it meant to become disengaged and lose trust in my employer. I became emotionally disconnected from my work, as if someone had flicked a switch. No matter how hard I tried to feel differently, it was too late. I had checked out and was ready to go elsewhere.

Once the psychological contract between manager and employee is broken, it will take Herculean effort to get things back on track. When you are leading in real time, you can ill afford creating a situation where trust is quickly eroded. Perception is reality, and a poor start to your working relationship will likely cause an irreparable rift.

Failed Onboarding

Imagine investing time, money, and energy to attract and recruit top talent but failing to plan the first days, weeks, and even months for your new hires at your organization? What do you think the results of that is? If you said disengagement, you'd be right.

Sadly, as it has for thousands of employees, disengagement often begins at the onboarding phase. If you're not doing all you can to inspire an individual to perform at their best at the outset, the chances are high that you've not only wasted your

Sadly, as it has
for thousands
of employees,
disengagement
often begins at the
onboarding phase.

———

time and efforts attracting them, but you've also sown the seeds for disenchantment from the first days on the job.

A recent Korn Ferry Futurestep survey[3] revealed that although almost all executives agreed that talent retention and mentorship are critical, about 25 percent of new hires leave within the first six months. And the main reason for doing so is that their role wasn't what they expected. What's interesting is that 69 percent of companies surveyed say they have a formal onboarding program in place for new employees. However, nearly a quarter of employees say that their program lasted *only one day*, and about a third said they lasted only for a week. How inspiring is that?

The onboarding phase is a critically important period for a new employee. They need to receive purposeful, well-thought-out orientation, and it needs to happen within the first 90 to 120 days. During this time, it's crucial that you establish performance benchmarks, connect new recruits with key personnel, provide hands-on training and support, build relationships, and help new hires acclimatize to the company culture. Do you have a strategy in place to welcome your new recruits? Expecting people to fend for themselves is reckless and irresponsible. In the absence of essential onboarding requirements, a new employee can easily become disengaged as soon as they are hired.

WHEN AN organization fails to set up a new hire for success in the early stages of their career, job dissatisfaction and ongoing turnover are likely consequences. The psychological contract is broken. And so it begins: HR departments and managers begin spinning their wheels in an effort to stop the cries of discontent, producing endless surveys aimed to flush out the source of the problem. All too often, however, the damage has already been done. Instead of addressing workplace culture, leadership, and broken systems, employees are mandated to answer questions that contribute to a heightened sense of frustration, lower morale, and further entrench a negative atmosphere. In short, solving employee engagement problems becomes far more complicated than necessary.

Proactive Solutions

To meet the new imperatives associated with leading and managing in real time, taking a proactive approach is a vital first step. Consider the possibilities of unearthing rich information regarding your employees by asking them to identify their biggest turnoffs at work. Chances are high that they will reveal some simple truths about their leadership, the workplace atmosphere, and how the big picture is conveyed.

Remember, no matter how challenging employee engagement may have become in your organization, it is a stretch to suggest that the majority of people show up at work with the intention to fail at their jobs. However, if the conditions required to inspire an individual to perform at their best do not exist, this is the root cause of most disengagement problems. The following solutions are effective and can help achieve full-fledged buy-in as long as your efforts are sincere.

Build Trust Immediately

Dr. Stephen R. Covey, author of *The 7 Habits of Highly Effective People*, famously stated that "trust is the highest form of motivation." When employees are micromanaged, they feel less inclined to apply additional discretionary effort. Mistrust compounds and disengagement builds when employees sense they are being controlled. Rather than *wanting* to complete a task willingly, a lack of trust creates a foreboding sense of employee *obligation* to get the work done. In other words, the willingness or desire to demonstrate additional discretionary effort dissipates and disengagement festers.

Use Analytics Wisely

Although survey data can yield quantitative information, it may still fail to provide an accurate snapshot of what is happening inside your organization. Departments may go to extraordinary lengths designing and implementing employment engagement surveys, but without full disclosure regarding how the information will be used, employees' concerns regarding confidentiality may result in lower than expected participation rates.

Ideally, surveys should result in *qualitative* value that will provide organizations with the information necessary to take concrete actions to improve discretionary effort.[4] Edgecumbe, a firm specializing in the links between leadership behaviors and performance outcomes, notes the following: "This type of research can help empower employees by giving them the platform to offer truly personal and truthful insights. When trying to build a successful team, understanding people's feelings and attitudes to company changes, leadership, and other pillars of operations, businesses can be equipped with the information they need." Remember, in order to obtain useful, qualitative information, you need to have already established a high-trust environment so that employees will want to share their perspectives openly. Your organization can glean invaluable information from intimate focus groups and informal group discussions, providing the right conditions exists.

Help New Recruits "Connect the Dots"

There is a direct correlation between effective onboarding programs, employee engagement, and retention. Companies that do not invest in meaningful, properly structured onboarding initiatives shouldn't be surprised when new employees quickly become confused regarding their role and place in the big picture. Any investments of valuable time, dollars, and energy used to attract and recruit talent will have been wasted when employees are left to sink or swim or, worse, leave because the purpose of their work and connection to your organizational vision was never made clear.

Your onboarding strategy must be well thought out and intentional. When your organization fails to set up a new hire for success in the early stages of their career, job dissatisfaction and ongoing turnover are likely consequences. Realize that the process of keeping people engaged can be improved by practicing preventative maintenance and making the appropriate arrangements for new employees to flourish from their first day on the job.

Prioritize the Intangible Motivators

People are attracted to an organization based on tangible offerings that include remuneration, benefits, and career-building opportunities. In the long run, however, they are more likely to stay when their value is acknowledged through genuine displays of trust, respect, camaraderie, and expressions of appreciation. These intangibles are indeed immeasurable and priceless aspects of your workplace culture and are key to engagement and retention. If you tend to this garden of intrinsic, non-financial motivators, the benefits may surprise you.

Eliminate Double Standards

Great wisdom on the topic of leading by example can be gleaned from the following words of the Greek philosopher Aristotle: "The worst form of inequality is trying to make unequal things equal." How is it possible to achieve higher levels of employee engagement when leaders aren't consistently modeling total commitment and positivity? Veronica, a former boss of mine that I introduced you to in Chapter 4, was consistently inconsistent. The more she blew hot and cold, the less inspired I became. It is the leader's responsibility to demonstrate the accountability they expect of their employees if they wish to encourage organization-wide engagement.

Reverse Mentoring

Examples abound of organizations that promote and implement reverse mentoring programs with high levels of success. This process of partnering senior leaders with younger employees has significant positive consequences on talent retention, engagement, and overall relationship dynamics. Jack Welch, the former CEO of General Electric who promoted reverse mentoring more than twenty years ago, described the activity as "tipping the organization upside down." Many renowned brands, including Estée Lauder, Target, AXA, Fidelity, and Cisco, have followed suit. As a result of embracing reverse mentoring, BNY Mellon's Pershing[5] experienced a staggering 96 percent retention rate for millennial participants. The intangible benefits that flow to the mentor and mentee can be profound. Both parties have a unique opportunity to forge stronger relationships by developing higher levels of trust and understanding in an informal, personal manner.

Another initiative exemplifying great partnerships between tenured leaders and new talent from some of the world's best schools and colleges is the worldwide success story known as CEOx1Day. Executive search and talent consulting company Odgers Berndtson popularized the idea of "uncovering, identifying and developing young leaders of tomorrow and matching them with innovative leaders of today."[6] The program has garnered publicity through traditional channels as well as through social media, building outstanding opportunities for mentees as well as mentors to harness deeper levels of understanding through a unique educational opportunity. More than a dozen countries are now participating in the program.

Mentorship through Delegation

Many leaders struggle with delegation, yet it is still considered to be a critical,[7] highly relevant skill. Employees respond positively to leaders who truly understand what it means to give them additional responsibilities. They don't want you to be a boss who passes the buck. Rather, they are looking to you as a mentor. Delegation is not abdication. Nor is it about giving employees the dirty work. Mentors share their experiences and help mentees learn in order to develop their skill sets. If you aren't willing to let go because you believe it is easier to do it yourself, you don't have a delegation problem—you have a trust problem and a need-to-control problem. Assigning responsibilities, when done correctly, can empower, inspire, and motivate people to excel in their role. And one of the greatest benefits when empowering others is building a more trusting relationship.

As more employees work remotely, leaders have an opportunity to change the dynamic by giving people greater autonomy and accountability to make decisions. By demonstrating belief in an individual's capability, a culture of trust will ensue. Allowing your team to do their best work in your absence is aspirational leadership at its finest.

WHEN I reflect on Philip and Ann's organization, I recognize that what fueled their success was their willingness to learn from their team. Leaders that do not encourage idea sharing may be setting themselves up for failure. The new workforce expects to be heard and places huge value on opportunities to collaborate. Many have brilliant suggestions or approaches that either lie dormant or are quashed simply because leaders have difficulty acknowledging the source. For some of them, the very thought of implementing ideas emanating from younger, smarter individuals represents a threat to the status quo as well as to their own position. The unfortunate result of that approach serves to exacerbate disengagement and accelerate the loss of valuable assets.

When employees feel emotionally invested in their work, their sense of pride and satisfaction deepens. The factors contributing to their high levels of engagement are largely driven by such intangibles as the workplace atmosphere and their immediate manager's level of trust, support, communication, and displays of appreciation. High engagement is inexorably tied to purposeful work and achieving mutual understanding regarding expectations. And isn't that what real-time leading is all about?

Real-Time Takeaways

- Leaders create a bond of trust from the moment information is shared, a task is assigned, or a job description is provided. Micromanagement and inconsistency can quickly break this bond and erode employee engagement.

- Focus on building dynamic employee experiences from day one. Develop onboarding programs that help new recruits quickly succeed with deliberate, genuine leadership interventions that foster engagement.

- Be open to learning from your team through reverse mentoring opportunities. These highly rewarding encounters are mutually beneficial when both parties experience collaboration and idea sharing in a less formal setting.

Real-Time Action Step

Inspired and motivated employees are highly engaged in their work. Identify one action, such as reviewing and strengthening your onboarding process regularly, that you and your leadership team can take to ensure that your workforce remains or becomes more engaged on a daily basis.

MEANING IS THE NEW MOTIVATION

"We have entered a new age of fulfillment, in which the great dream is to trade up from money to meaning."

ROMAN KRZNARIC

I RECALL helping a group of supervisors in the pharmaceutical industry to become more effective leaders. During a workshop, one participant lamented the fact that her team members were required to do so-called menial work. When I asked her to explain the work in more detail, she described the specific process required to prepare test tubes for experiments in her laboratory such as sterilizing, labeling, and categorizing. Her comment and use of the word *menial* provoked a fascinating discussion. As we pondered the expression and purpose of her team's work, I asked the group to think about how we attach negative connotation to work that is labeled *menial*. What do you think the response of the team may have been if the supervisor had focused on the importance of the work in the grand scheme of the company's success? What would happen if there was no team to prepare the test tubes? Would other departments be able to work effectively without her team's support? This supervisor, who was tasked with the responsibility of ensuring the highest standards were adhered to throughout the test tube preparation process, experienced a lightbulb moment: she realized that she could communicate the *value* of her team's work in a positive way and change their expectations of it at the same time.

This story illustrates the potential to shift the dynamic between a leader and their team through management of expectation. Although some tasks may be repetitive and hum-drum, a leader's influence regarding how and why such work is important can make a world of difference to their team. It *is* possible to create greater ownership when a leader is more cognizant of their words, mannerisms, and beliefs regarding the meaning and purpose of the work.

ARE YOU excited about the work that your team performs on a daily basis?

The chances are high that if you aren't conveying enthu-siasm and sincere interest in the value of their work, your employees are picking up on your overall vibe. Dan Cable, pro-fessor of organizational behavior at the London Business School, calls this *emotions projection*.[1] When a leader exhibits negative behavior toward his team's work, it has a heavy impact on oppor-tunities for creativity and innovation now and in the future.

As we strive for greater meaning in our day-to-day lives, the delineation between work and life purpose has become increasingly blurred. We no longer need to go to work to do work. And many organizations are recognizing that their workforce are now expecting a meaningful exchange for their time. Leaders who can successfully demonstrate the ultimate purpose of every department and every individual within their respective team, and are also able to achieve buy-in, have indeed discovered the secret of employee motivation and retention.

Explain the Benefits

When the connection between an individual's contribution and purpose of their efforts is clear, the sky is the limit. Jackie Norman, CEO of Safety Services Nova Scotia, states it simply: "We need to collaborate, work in teams, listen to ideas. Newer generations taking part in our student work initiatives work differently to how we did. This involves teamwork, being included, valued, and having their ideas heard. Leaders need to take time to ask questions and to really listen, which is the key, and find out what is important to them, i.e., their values such as protecting the environment and prioritizing health and wellness. Let them take on these projects. That gives them a purpose and a goal that is near and dear to them."

When you engage your workforce, though, you also need to manage the expectations you create. And that begins by making sure your employees understand the why behind their work. Nothing is more off-putting to an employee than trying to discern the meaning behind your words.

The responsibility of communicating the *why* aspect of a task lies with the leader. Ideally, stories such as Norman's should be more commonplace. I have lost count of the times employees have shared stories with me about a lack of direction or clear intent shown by their immediate manager, supervisor, or senior leadership. In addition, leaders often underestimate the value of clarifying objectives for teams so that they can be successful. When supporting younger teams, some leaders may feel threatened by their initiative and so avoid discussing objectives altogether, leaving the team hanging.

First and foremost, if you truly want employees to take ownership of their work, explain the benefits from *their* perspective. Think about a time when you were asked to do a particular task and found yourself left in the dark, trying to figure out what to do and why it was important. Perhaps you felt frustrated or sensed that you were a mere cog in the wheel? When the employee/employer relationship is purely transactional, the work is void of meaning. Conversely, when a manager clearly articulates the purpose of a task or project and demonstrates the value of the individual's contribution, the task or project takes on greater meaning.

Your Motive Counts

Organizations that understand the value of their workforce during good times as well as tough times will always be desirable places to work. Businesses in an array of market sectors demonstrated extraordinary leadership during the COVID-19 pandemic. We witnessed numerous examples of CEOs and senior leadership forgoing salaries and taking immediate action to ensure that the health and financial well-being of their employees were their highest priority. *Forbes*[2] showcased the efforts of Allied Financial Services, a company with almost nine thousand staff, highlighting their quick response to the crisis by providing them with financial assistance, access to mental health professionals, full coverage for diagnostic testing related to the virus, as well as many other outstanding initiatives. There is little doubt that Allied's real-time actions will be remembered by the staff and their families for years to come.

During the pandemic, *meaningful work* took on a vastly different connotation. Many blue-collar jobs in grocery stores, wholesale distribution centers, and assembly lines associated with vital supply chains were sought after. The world's largest auto makers, distilleries, and perfume and cosmetics factories switched gears and transformed their assembly lines to support the massive demand for ventilators, masks, hand sanitizer, disinfectants, and critical medical equipment. Sports stadiums, cruise ships, navy vessels, hotels, concert halls, and convention centers became hospitals and triage facilities. Many businesses and individuals stepped up to help people who live alone. Restaurants and private citizens prepared meals at no charge. We witnessed numerous acts of kindness from people wanting to make a difference by delivering food to those on the frontlines in healthcare, the elderly, and others in their communities who were struggling to take care of themselves.

In contrast, the actions of some businesses drew public attention for the wrong reasons. For example, a number of television commercials appeared almost overnight to show support for their employees or healthcare professionals, patriotic attempts to showcase brands during a time of crisis. The ads were received with skepticism, as many perceived them as disingenuous, rather than portraying a sense of truly caring for humankind.

When an organization's values, words, and actions are authentically aligned, workers respond accordingly. There is a direct correlation between empowerment and intrinsically rewarding work. When people feel that they are performing meaningful work, their commitment and engagement levels rise proportionately. Today's workforce has a heightened awareness of their employer's values. Similar to millennials, Gen Zers pay close attention to the motives of leaders within organizations as well as the causes they support, both being important considerations to these generations when assessing their vocation options.

There is a direct
correlation between
empowerment
and intrinsically
rewarding work.

————

Deloitte's most recent annual Global Millennial Survey, "A Generation Disrupted," points to higher levels of distrust among the younger generations because they are "caught in the crossfire of societal, political, and economic commotion."[3] The survey also notes that the effects of radical changes that began during the world financial crisis of late 2007 to mid-2009 have had a major psychological impact on Generation Z in particular, a cohort that has spent "half of their lives in a post-crash world."

This is significantly different to the boomer experience. As the word implies, boom times were characterized by economic opportunity and expansive growth. But higher levels of financial distress have created a shift in priorities for Generation X. Unlike their grandparents before them, accomplishments such as home ownership and raising a family do not hold the same meaning. Experiences such as traveling the globe or contributing to their local community have higher relevance and importance. Their level of consciousness regarding societal disparities and their political rhetoric influence their habits as consumers and their employment choices. They are attracted to businesses and employers whose values are in sync with theirs. The Deloitte Global Millennial Survey Executive Summary[4] aptly captures the long-term aspirations for both employers and their workforce: "The organizations that can make the future brighter for millennials and Gen Zs stand to have the brightest futures themselves."

It's Not Just the Paycheck

To say that all workplaces are not created equal is an oversimplification. Many people do work for the paycheck. Receiving financial compensation in exchange for performing work makes perfect sense if we are going to sustain ourselves and our families. Over the years I have had many discussions with leaders and teams about whether people simply show up because they *have* to (if they wish to be paid), or whether there is a deeper reason. Some have fervently argued that it's only about the paycheck. I disagree.

Leaders who have a narrow view regarding the exchange of labor for pay are missing the point. If you choose to believe that people are simply punching the clock because they view work as a transaction, it may be worthwhile to challenge your own assumptions and consider the impact of your leadership style and your organization's culture. Is your workplace an inspiring place to be? Employees can be energized or disheartened by their environment and leadership. When people sense indifference on the part of leaders and managers, it is a major turnoff. The paycheck can quickly become irrelevant.

I have been privy to many woeful tales regarding leaders and managers who suck the life out of their people by treating them poorly. And, more alarmingly, doing so with very little consciousness. I recall one such relationship with a senior leader early in my leadership career that caused me to reevaluate my position entirely. I had become disconnected and disillusioned with my work and ultimately decided to leave an organization I once loved. My own act of clock punching and my mechanical approach to my work had nothing to do with collecting pay and everything to do with a complete loss of passion and motivation to stay. A series of unrelenting negative experiences can wear people down to the point of no return.

Leaders now and in the future need to positively increase their influence and motivate their employees to self-actualize. In the face of uncertainty, complexity, and increasing competition for talent, the "little things" can't be overlooked by leaders. To borrow a term from author and global business thinker Tamara J. Erickson, "Meaning is the new money."[5]

If you want your team to bring the very best of themselves to work, recognize that how you show up is a significant part of *their* success equation.

Subtract the Demotivators

Money isn't the only reason for people to put in an appearance at work. If leaders are willing and able to dig deeper, they can identify, remove, and replace the following tangibles and intangibles that contribute to an employee's lack of desire or increasing disinterest in their work.

Work as Drudgery

Leaders who bring out the best in their teams often challenge them to perform tasks that they could not imagine doing. For example, Michael Campbell, the custodial services manager mentioned in Chapter 3, was able to get his team to participate in a series of highly successful safety videos. Not only did they enjoy the experience, but they also eagerly lined up to get involved! Michael was able to achieve buy-in to key safety initiatives by getting his staff excited about their contribution. He succeeded because he had previously established trust, rapport, and unwavering loyalty.

Punishing Good Performance

For decades, leaders have debated the notion that cash is the biggest employee perk. Leaders falsely assume that a workplace motivator is to reward hard work with more work. Although some individuals may want to work longer hours, it is a mistake to believe that all individuals share these values regarding money. Employees have different priorities that vary based on demographics as well as lifestyle choices. Some place a higher value on flexible hours, working from home, or nonfinancial incentives, such as recognition or special project opportunities. Any discussion regarding overtime or additional hours needs to be exactly that, a conversation.

Lack of Appreciation

Despite the continuing paradigm changes in technology, culture, and demographics in our workplaces, people remain fundamentally driven by recognition and appreciation. Citing every piece of research that supports this fact would be a difficult mission. Whatever tasks your team carries out, regardless of whether they go above and beyond what is expected, people want to be noticed, recognized, and validated. Appreciation is the highest form of motivation. Showing meaningful acknowledgment through words and actions goes a long way toward inspiring people to achieve their goals. The effort required is minimal; however, the benefits are significant. These will be evident in your metrics such as lower turnover, higher productivity, reduced absenteeism, and the bottom line.

Micromanagement

It's hard to believe that Michael Gerber's famous book, *The E Myth*, was first published in 1986. Why do leaders still find it so difficult to let go of control, insisting on doing what Gerber described as working *in* rather than *on* their businesses? Logically, we know that attempts to direct all the minutiae, the intricacies of every employee's job, is futile. Leaders can, and should, be managing their time more effectively. Yet, for many leaders, delegating the details and allowing people to manage themselves and their work are anxiety-inducing exercises. This practice of meddling remains rampant, despite the emotional harm it causes and the associated risk of permanently damaging the employee/employer relationship.

FOR MANY employees, finding meaning in daily tasks has transcended workplace boundaries. Recent events have galvanized people from all age groups and diverse backgrounds as they seek a deeper purpose and desire to contribute, not only to their workplace but beyond. Social media has made the world a smaller place as people can now connect from virtually any place on the planet, in real time. Information regarding a host of social causes is available instantaneously. For some employees, disengagement from work and management is now being channeled as discontentment with the status quo and with a multitude of issues that affect their fellow citizens of the world. Local issues can quickly and potentially escalate to global concerns within a matter of seconds, so real-time leaders must be ready to respond in a meaningful way.

Real-Time Takeaways

- When a leader doesn't express the value and meaning of an employee's work, that leader is neglecting a powerful, intangible motivator. Employees *want* to feel connected to your organization's purpose and respond positively when you reinforce their connection to the big picture.

- Although a monetary reward is one form of showing appreciation, regular expression of authentic recognition resonates on a deeper level.

- When you offer employees additional financial compensation for working longer hours, you may also be establishing a culture that rewards hard work with more work.

- Trust is the antidote to control. Empowering others and allowing them to succeed will always be a real-time leadership attribute.

Real-Time Action Step

There is a correlation between meaningful work, appreciation, and engagement. As you reflect on this chapter, think about whether your workforce receives sufficient genuine acknowledgment for their contribution to your organization's purpose. What, if anything, could you and your leaders do differently?

VOICES RISING

"I think the greatest sound in the world is the sound of the human voice."

MILES DAVIS

IN APRIL 2019, Amazon employees opened a Twitter account Amazon Employees for Climate Justice (@AMZNforClimate) that garnered a following of more than twelve thousand people. Their posts not only addressed their employer's position on climate change but also drew attention to other employers regarding their stance on safe working conditions, climate change, and systemic racism.

The Amazon employee group has been effective in their efforts to capture worldwide attention, including that of Amazon's CEO, Jeff Bezos, and the senior leadership on the issue of climate change. They staged numerous walkouts and protests that were covered by traditional media on an ongoing basis. In addition, the group successfully enlisted the support of other tech industry employees on the issue as well as other social causes.

Just prior to the UN climate change summit in 2019, Amazon announced its Climate Pledge,[1] committing to the goal of reaching net-zero carbon emissions by 2040, as well as using 100 percent renewable energy throughout the company by 2030. The pledge was directly linked to the efforts of the employee climate group whose views are now considered to be shared by a large number of Americans, according to a study[2] by the Yale Program on Climate Change Communication.

Throughout 2020, workers in multiple Amazon locations worldwide walked off the job in support of coworkers who had spoken out about their work environment. At the time, COVID-19 was spreading quickly, and the workers cited safety fears, a lack of protective equipment, and the negative reaction from leadership as their reason for leaving their job posts.

The company's response was twofold. Employees received warnings following their criticism of company policy, an action that only spurred additional debate and division. At the same time, Amazon also issued updates on their corporate blog, listed their initiatives, and reiterated their concern for the health and well-being of all staff. These initiatives included ramping up their investment in resources to keep team members safe. Amazon also paid out thank-you bonuses and established a $25 million relief fund for delivery drivers and seasonal workers who were experiencing hardship. And they hired almost 200,000 new staff to expediate shipping and delivery of millions of items to their customers during the pandemic.

Clearly, the Amazon employee Twitter account is making a difference for workers and doesn't appear to be losing its influence. When last I checked the account, in January of 2021, its followers had grown to over twelve thousand and the account holders continue to post frequently.

TODAY'S WORKERS are sending a strong message to leaders, demanding they act beyond the company's walls. Findings from an extensive study by the international law firm Herbert Smith Freehills reveal that 80 percent of companies predict a rise in workforce activism with 95 percent expecting an increase in workers' use of social media to amplify their voice. At the same time, employers who are competing for talent are finding that social activism, both internal and external, could negatively impact their reputation and global revenues by 25 percent annually, especially if they choose to ignore these voices.[3]

Numerous enterprises now recognize the urgent and prudent business case for pursuing and engraining a sustainability policy. As Michael Bloomberg states in the Bloomberg Impact Report[4] released in 2020, "As governments in every region pursue policies to get their economies back on solid footing, we have an unprecedented opportunity to make smart investments that accelerate our transition to a 100 percent clean energy economy and lay the foundation for strong and sustainable growth in the years ahead."

But the workforce is also paying close attention to corporate statements on these issues of clean energy and sustainable growth, notably the correlation between rhetoric and tangible action. This means that one of the best courses of action for employers is to be fully cognizant of employee values and beliefs and to take steps to improve their understanding about what matters to their workforce and why.

The Shifting Balance of Power

The impact of social networks is immense. Huge numbers of people now have a voice and aren't hesitant to use it. Any individual at any time and from any location can express their opinion about any subject. Within a matter of seconds, a message can be broadcast, shared, and reshared worldwide in different media. This single change matters for leaders because the workforce can now communicate their perspectives, opinions, and experiences far beyond their cubicles or assembly lines.

Employees can instantly tell the world how they feel about you or their workplace and have no qualms about telling their CEOs what they think either. They don't want or need to wait for permission to use the supposed correct channels in order to get attention from the top, especially if they aren't getting any traction internally. For example, in 2018, over four thousand Google employees vigorously opposed their company's plans to collaborate with the US government on an AI project known as Project Maven, to study drone footage. They petitioned Sundar Pichai, CEO of Alphabet Inc., Google's parent company, and eventually the project was canned. In 2019, once again thousands of employees voiced their displeasure over Google's plans to bid on a cloud contract[5] with the US customs and border agency, signing a petition highlighting breaches of human rights and international law standards by the agency. Work and social causes are no longer separate conversations. People freely discuss what causes matter to them personally while they are at work. They express their ideas because they are part of a global community. Not only do they expect to be heard, but they also expect leaders to act. And if they see no action on the part of their employers, they will continue to use their voices to create change.

One issue that has gathered a multitude of voices is systemic racial injustice. A deep and thorough discussion of this subject is far beyond the confines of this book, but it must be mentioned in context of the responsiveness of senior leadership. The killing of George Floyd on May 25, 2020, gal-vanized people around the world in the fight against systemic racial injustice. It triggered an unprecedented corporate response within the US in particular, highlighting the need for organizations to address their own inadequate stances on diversity and inclusion. Internal and external pressures have thrown the spotlight on responses from senior leadership to the killing of Floyd, as stakeholders, employees, and cus-tomers paid particularly close attention to the authenticity of their messaging.

Unsurprisingly, surveys reveal[6] that employees from differ-ent backgrounds and demographics have divergent opinions regarding whether or not their organizations view discrimi-nation overall as a problem within their workplace and in American workplaces in general. Specifically, African-American and younger workers feel that their workplaces and work-places in general could do more. Leaders who aren't aware of the impact of discriminatory practices are putting their cus-tomer and employee brands at risk. There is no exception to this new reality. Employees expect their leaders at all levels to be exemplary human beings with a heightened understand-ing of what it means to truly accept and embrace *all* peoples.

The list of employees calling on their leadership to act in the face of racism is substantial and growing. The outpouring of grief and anger over Floyd's death and the actions of the police also prompted employees at the Ford Motor Company to write to CEO[7] Jim Hackett asking that the company, the largest manufacturer of police vehicles in the US, to stop selling to police. And this was just one example among many of note at the time of writing this book:

- Facebook CEO Mark Zuckerberg came under fire[8] from members of his senior leadership and employees regarding a post pertaining to then President Donald Trump's stance on rioting, looting, and the police response.

- Twelve hundred employees sent a letter calling for "seven acts of change"[9] to the Centers for Disease Control and Prevention's director, Robert Redfield, asking him to address ongoing racism at the CDC.

- Christene Barberich, cofounder and editor in chief at Refinery29, an American multinational digital media and entertainment website, departed[10] in response to accusations of a toxic work culture.

- Ian Shugart, clerk of the Privy Council and secretary to the Cabinet, Government of Canada, penned a call to action[11] for greater diversity within the public service.

- A grassroots revolt[12] related to diversity issues at AT&T Inc.'s Bleacher Report offices led to the departure of CEO Howard Mittman.

Apart from leaders being called out by their employees to stamp out racism within their own walls, corporate boards are also scrutinized even more closely regarding their overall lack of diversity. No matter how many senior leaders make public pronouncements committing to do more to remedy the problem, authentic and lasting action remains elusive. It is foolhardy to think that systemic racism remains a major issue in North America alone. This is a global problem in business, politics, and everyday life. Amid the double standards, platitudes, hypocrisy, and skepticism around companies' ability to make meaningful change, one thing is true: voices continue to rise boldly and loudly.

The real-time leader looks for ways to gain deeper insight into their employees' hunger to make a difference.

———

The Meaningful Alternative

In September 2019, while on my way to a client meeting in downtown Vancouver, I noticed a large gathering taking place several streets away. Thousands of school children and adults protested in unison regarding climate change. Simultaneous events were taking place around the world, inspired by Greta Thunberg, the sixteen-year-old Swedish climate activist who founded a global movement. Thunberg, who has appeared on the cover of *Time* magazine as Person of the Year, has addressed the World Economic Forum, the United Nations, and US Congress, sharing her message that climate change must be dealt with here and now.

Although climate change and greenhouse emissions have been a concern since the first industrial revolution, the debate has dramatically shifted in recent times from a small group of eco-warriors to the much broader public. In many instances, the narrative is now driven by employees in younger demographics who are prioritizing their career choices based on prospective employers' stance on this issue.

Like Greta Thunberg, there are many young activists who are inspiring change on several key fronts, both within and outside their workplaces. By using their voices to articulate their opinions on key social issues, they are successfully causing organizations to be more introspective and accountable. But problems arise when antiquated channels of internal communication are still in place, or employers resist entering into a dialogue to address their employees' concerns. The alternative to unrest and dissatisfaction within your workforce is for leaders to expand opportunities for greater engagement and dialogue. The real-time leader looks for ways to gain deeper insight into their employees' hunger to make a difference. Some leaders misconstrue displays of passion and desire for change as iconoclasm. But when dissonance exists, listening to and acknowledging divergent opinions, even if you disagree, is the prudent course of action. Try these strategies to forge stronger, trusting relationships with your workforce.

1   **Harness a global mindset and increased social awareness.** This skill is applicable in a variety of contexts. It is no longer enough for leaders to be thinking about their organization from a local or national perspective. The accessibility of technology and information has brought the world closer. That means employees expect leaders to sharpen their awareness of global trends and issues that include sustainability, climate change, mental health, economic and social disparities, shifting workforce demographics, and the gig economy, to name a few.

2   **Meet on neutral ground.** Whether you choose to call them forums or town halls, your employees welcome opportunities for increased dialogue. As mentioned previously, people have an inherent desire to feel psychologically safe (p. 112) and will respond positively when they feel heard and understood. More can be accomplished when a discussion takes place on neutral territory. By removing the "us versus them" adversarial scenarios, you can create an environment for deeper discussion, trust, and respect.

3   **Increase transparency.** It is difficult to make progress when leadership conversations regarding organizational values are shrouded in secrecy. When the workforce calls for transparency, this is not the time for leadership to be unavailable, to exhibit frustration, or to go on the defensive. These responses serve no one. Greater transparency builds higher levels of trust, especially when difficult topics arise.

4 **Narrow the perception gap.** For many years, leaders and teams have struggled to be on the same page regarding how they see each other. There is a persistent perception gap between what leaders *think* their employees need to be motivated and engaged at work—what leaders think they are providing—and what those workers *actually* need. With so much discussion around heightened social consciousness on a global scale, it is incumbent on leaders to narrow the gap by forging stronger relationships and recognizing that their workforce truly sees themselves as citizens of the world.

THROUGHOUT THE course of history, workers and employers have clashed on a host of issues, including working conditions, inequities in pay, unfair dismissals, and sexual harassment, to name just a few. Only now, the voices being raised can be amplified much more quickly, and the failure to listen can result in dire consequences to your organization's reputation as well as your personal credibility. Your business depends on paying attention to the rising voices and taking ownership to resolve concerns and practice greater accountability.

Remember that taking action in real time is often *the* best time. The power of an immediate response to the needs of your team is that it contributes significantly to an atmosphere of greater mutual understanding and respect.

Real-Time Takeaways

➤ Employee activism within and outside of your organization's walls is on the rise. Tangible evidence indicates that a passive response will have an adverse effect on corporate revenue.

➤ Employees expect alignment between organizational values and actions. It is your responsibility to demonstrate consistency and awareness regarding your stance on societal issues and trends.

➤ Rising voices are an opportunity to drive change and create more dialogue. Your employees are your most significant asset, and it is in your best interest to foster an open, transparent culture rather than impose draconian, reactive HR policies.

➤ Taking a positive position on social causes that matter to your workforce and society at large will enhance your employer and customer brand.

Real-Time Action Step

Review the four strategies for forging stronger, more trusting relationships with your workforce. Choose one that resonates for discussion and easy application among your leadership team. Your goal is to deepen your understanding and perspective regarding issues that matter to your employees while creating opportunities for dialogue.

THE DEMAND FOR ACCOUNTABILITY

9

"The right thing to do and the hard thing to do are usually the same."

STEVE MARABOLI

I WILL never forget the day that my boss, Greg, summoned me into his office just before Christmas. I was living in Australia at the time and the weather was hot and humid. Many people hit the beach after work and, on that day, that was my plan too.

At the time the economy was in a recession, and I knew the downturn would hit the business hard. I was also relatively new to the company, having worked there for less than a year. Last one in; first one out. Greg broke the bad news quickly, callously, and unexpectedly. He was letting me go to "free me up for new opportunities." His words rang hollow, void of understanding and empathy. I was told to pack up my belongings and leave the office immediately. All my hopes were shattered in an instant, and I felt crushed as my head flooded with fears about the future. I had no idea how I would manage.

It didn't help that I had to hurriedly empty the contents of my company car and leave it behind. The trunk contained an assortment of beach gear that I had to haul into the bar where I met a friend to commiserate and process what had just happened. Suddenly, I was trying to come to grips with being unemployed. I never saw Greg again, although I learned that six months later his company folded. Although my experience occurred over thirty years ago, I will always remember how that experience made me feel, especially as it took me four long months to find another job.

It's Complicated

Leaders everywhere are under greater pressure to show strength, tenacity, inspiration, and hope, especially in times of crisis and uncertainty. Leaders will always need to make difficult decisions, but remaining cognizant of how you do so is part of the job. That's because all decisions, including how you terminate staff, have ramifications. Today, people expect accountability from their leaders, a reality that isn't likely to change anytime soon.

Accountability comes with the territory, so leaders often feel that they are under a microscope. Sure, others may be responsible for getting the work done, but you as the leader are ultimately responsible for the outcome. Although there is no question that mastering leadership accountability involves making certain that your employees know exactly where their responsibilities start and end, leadership accountability has new and more complex dimensions.

Let's consider the demand for greater accountability from two vantage points: first, in the light of the recent COVID-19 crisis, followed by a deeper look at the connection between credibility and accountability and why it matters.

In 2020 the phrase "unprecedented times" was used more frequently (and some would say annoyingly) than any other to describe the current state of the world. Some prefer a different expression to encapsulate the impact of the pandemic, incorporating "Miss Rona,"[1] or "The Rona" into their lexicon. These are slang terms coined by Gen Z as an alternative to their medical counterpart, COVID-19. As we attempted to figure out solutions to survive the economic downturn and devasting health crisis caused by Miss Rona, global leaders in politics and business felt her wrath in a multitude of ways.

Many employees were furloughed, either temporarily or permanently, due to the pandemic, and how they felt when their leader broke the news is not something easily forgotten. This is also the case if there is an economic downturn, a merger, or any other kind of global event that necessitates the letting go of staff. Whatever the cause, even if there was no alternative, leaders may find themselves haunted by an employee's experience of the termination should they find themselves needing to replace that employee's skills in due course. In these situations, approach matters a great deal. And a leader's actions are being evaluated, even by those who are personally unaffected by them, as a reflection of your employer brand.[2]

The pandemic highlighted the importance of leaders needing to be the best version of themselves. While the global community reeled from the economic and social impacts, leaders in both small and large enterprises had a unique opportunity to show their teams what matters most during uncertain times, which is consistent, caring, and compassionate real-time communication. A delayed response could easily be misconstrued as disinterest or a lack of sensitivity.

Leaders who demonstrate empathy, authenticity, and transparency will be in a stronger position when better times return. For those who are not cognizant of the psychological impact of a crisis on their people, their most valuable asset, the repercussions to their business and bottom line may be worse than the crisis itself.

There is no question that business owners face difficult and harsh truths when struggling to stay afloat. At the same time, experience tells me that the human side of leadership (p. 81) is sorely needed during good times and bad. The right words and actions speak loudly. Leaders can build accountability and mitigate the personal anguish felt by employees during a crisis when they choose to practice the following behaviors.

Acknowledge fear and anxiety. When people are unexpectedly thrown into a new reality, often they feel hopeless. It is understandable that the possibility of losing their livelihood would dominate their thoughts. Whether our fears and anxieties are real or imagined, a leader's role is to be supportive by acknowledging these feelings and allowing others to express them openly, prior to offering any solutions.

Show empathy and understanding. If you have ever experienced the impact of an economic downturn or any kind of hardship, your words of wisdom can be a great comfort. But it is important not to try to make yourself the "hero." People want you to relate your own personal challenge to help give context to their troubles and demonstrate that what they are feeling is perfectly normal. Invincibility in the face of extremely difficult circumstances is an impossible state of being for most humans. When you are emotionally available, you create opportunities to build stronger relationships. If a team member feels comfortable enough to share their pain in confidence, it is a testament to the fact that they trust you; your authenticity is resonating at a deep level.

Convey reassurance. We gravitate toward positive energy and encouraging words, especially from individuals we respect and trust. During uncertain times, one of the most important roles that a leader can play is to share messages of hope. As the COVID-19 pandemic escalated and news of the rising death toll was broadcast daily, the world looked to its leaders for inspiration. A leader is uniquely positioned to give comfort and show strength. I will even argue that they are charged with this responsibility as part of the job description.

Model resilience. The capacity to be resilient and recover from a series of expected or unexpected changes is an increasingly sought-after competency in leaders. Those who anticipate and are attuned to the inevitability of disruption can help their teams proactively respond and rise above the shock factors commonly associated with a crisis. The pandemic represented an opportunity for leaders to show more humanity, build relationships, and demonstrate positive influence. Some leaders opted to stay connected to those workers who were laid off and checked in with them personally, inquiring about their health and their family's well-being. Some opted to be the first person at the door, wearing a face mask and distributing hand sanitizer as they welcomed people back into the workplace. Whatever the circumstances are, your actions during a crisis shine a spotlight on both your leadership style and your organization's reputation.

During uncertain times, one of the most important roles that a leader can play is to share messages of hope.

The Link between Credibility and Accountability

Now that we've considered the vantage point of why credibility is important, it's easy to see why being conscious of how your actions are perceived is a worthwhile endeavor. The frequency of prominent public figures coming under scrutiny is nothing new. However, the advent of social media and its immediate accessibility provide the world with an instantaneous portrayal of leaders in compromising circumstances. Not a day passes without a reference to a leader's fall from grace somewhere on the planet (see the examples in Chapter 8). News regarding the behaviors of a politician or a corporate executive's transgressions can spark outrage from a world that seems to relish sensationalism, no matter how ugly, scandalous, true, or false. Headlines laden with allegations of misdemeanors that include misappropriated use of company or government expense accounts, fraudulent spending of taxpayer funds, drug addiction, marital affairs, lies, and corruption of some form or another continue to demand our attention. When confronted with their assortment of character flaws, denial seems to be the easier option for the accused.

The underlying concern is the speculation that such leaders generate as a result of their questionable activities and the implications for their employer and consumer brands. We look to our leaders as positive examples and become profoundly disappointed. The display of deceit by those that we uphold as role models as they dance around the truth defies logic, yet it has become the norm. When we witness bad behavior on the part of our leaders, it causes us to reflect on our own standards and, in many cases, helps determine where we choose to work and for whom.

Now, imagine a leader making the news for the right reasons. A leader who upholds integrity as a core value. Fortunately, such exemplary individuals *do* exist, although many are quietly going about their business without fanfare, so we don't hear about them as often. They do not need the accolades or public adulation because this leadership characteristic goes hand in hand with humility (p. 18) and integrity. Brian Tracy, chairman and CEO of Brian Tracy International, describes integrity[3] as "doing the right thing because it's the right thing to do."

Spearheading any enterprise requires strength of character, especially when a decision to go in a particular direction has costly consequences for the bottom line and for employees' livelihoods. When a leader chooses the wrong path, they are ultimately responsible, even if the decisions were made in consultation with others on an executive team or board of directors. Taking steps from the following sections will help you get to that place of ultimate credibility.

Improve Your Accountability Quotient

In Chapter 3, I introduced you to Michael Campbell, the manager of custodial services of Dalhousie University (p. 64) who transformed the safety culture within his workforce. Michael models many of the characteristics that have helped him build a culture of positive accountability. His safety videos and curriculum, which have since been rolled out to other universities and businesses in Nova Scotia, were built by allowing for divergent opinions. Under Michael's leadership, supervisors felt comfortable to express alternative ways to make their program successful. One supervisor with more than thirty years on the job suggested that the videos be kept simple so their diverse workforce, whose first language was not English, could easily follow and buy in. Michael listened. He acknowledges that others had ideas that were better than his own.

Michael passionately believes that people come to work because they are attracted to the organization and what it represents but stay for the leader and the culture. In his words, "People work for people. If you don't have leaders that people want to work for, you have nothing." His department's safety record is a testament to his leadership style that encourages transparency and personal accountability.

Accountability starts with you. But not all leaders are able to recognize when they have a *me* problem rather than a *we* problem. As I talked about in Chapter 8, a leader who is mindful of employee activism and the benefits of a consultative approach with their workforce will foster stronger relationships and boost their organization's reputation. How many of the statements in the following list apply to you?

- I am a leader who admits when the organization has taken a wrong turn.

- I am a leader who takes swift action when hearing of unacceptable behavior by any team member, at any level.

- I am a leader who knows how to address individual issues without causing embarrassment to others.

- I am a leader who willingly steps in to help.

- I am a leader who does not place themself above others.

- I am a leader whom others can count on.

- I am a leader who is thoughtful.

- I am a leader who is respectful.

- I am a leader who doesn't take all the credit.

- I am a leader who lives their values.

- I am a leader who models consistency.

Now, can you identify areas where there is room for improvement? Making an effort to acknowledge if you are not as strong in some areas as others, followed by an earnest desire to improve, will help you raise your accountability quotient.

Credibility Killers

A job title does not signify instant credibility. The truth is credibility has nothing to do with position and power and everything to do with consistency, integrity, and accountability in action. We admire individuals who are not only clear about their values but live them on a daily basis. And we hold leaders accountable by assessing whether their words are backed up by their actions.

When we tell others that we value great workplace relationships, are we demonstrating this core belief in all our interactions? We acquire a positive reputation by being values-based in everything we do. Imagine the possibilities if we all committed to saying what we mean and meaning what we say. Values not only drive our behavior, but they also drive an organization's purpose. The importance of a leader's credibility is inexorably linked to the workplace atmosphere. In the eyes of those they lead, the following credibility issues are absolute killers.

Egomaniacal Leadership

Humility is one of the most appealing leadership traits (p. 18). It is the equalizer in business relationships because it humanizes the dynamic between a leader and an employee. Some leaders mistakenly believe that by revealing their foibles, they become overly transparent. Conversely, a leader who lacks humility is often perceived as self-indulgent, self-serving, and even narcissistic—a major turnoff for your workforce. Authors Edgar A. Schein and Peter H. Schein[4] contend that in order for organizations to thrive, they must demonstrate the nimbleness and creativity that can only be achieved by "humble leadership" at every level.

Broken Promises

A leader who is not true to their word will quickly lose respect because broken promises rarely go unremembered. I once worked for an organization whose CEO reneged on a promise to my manager to honor my employment contract and provide me with a company vehicle. When the CEO finally relented six months later, I'd already lost faith in the company, passion for my work, and belief in the leader's vision that I'd initially bought into. Attempts to backpedal in the aftermath of such gaffes often result in greater damage to a leader's credibility. A slew of broken promises slowly chips away at a leader's and an organization's track record, overshadowing or potentially erasing previous good-news stories.

Public Put-Downs

Up until relatively recently, a coach in almost any sport could call out a player, or an entire team, for poor performance using humiliation as a tactic to inspire motivation. The same was true for business, though it's unclear whether this has a demonstrable motivational effect. When leaders resort to this strategy it is not only considered unacceptable, but it can also generate significant economic repercussions. If you have ever experienced being publicly berated by a leader, you probably remember the denigrating episode as if it happened yesterday. Regardless of whether an employee is experiencing difficulty with their work, no one expects to be embarrassed in front of their peers. There is no excuse for a pejorative, public display of displeasure regarding employee performance, or any situation where others are blamed for your own mistakes. As writer John Hamm[5] eloquently puts it, "If you want to know why so many organizations sink into chaos, look no further than their leaders' mouths."

Breach of Trust

Do you ask your employees or contractors to sign a confidentiality document when they come on board? And do you apply this same trust requirement to yourself and others on your leadership team? Without question, one of the most disappointing and gut-wrenching experiences is learning that a candid, confidential conversation with a leader did not remain private. When an executive is witness to the disclosure of an employee's personal problem or extremely sensitive matter and subsequently breaches their trust, the hurt caused may be irreparable; the negative consequences to engagement, your culture, and overall morale may be even worse. News travels faster than ever these days; when a leader's betrayal goes viral, there is nowhere to hide.

A Culture of No Accountability

Taking ownership starts from the top. Managers and teams are mindful of double standards and expect the leader to recognize that they are ultimately accountable for establishing the direction and vision of the organization. When leaders sanction a lack of responsibility regarding decision-making as well as results that aren't acceptable, they have failed to grasp that the onus of responsibility rests with them.

People expect leaders to take charge, whether they are tasked with making unpalatable yet necessary personnel changes, reining in costs, or delivering bad news. Remember Bill in Chapter 4, who abdicated the responsibility to his managers? Leaders who balk at taking actions that may be unpopular are permitting others to do the same, thereby tarnishing their own reputation. Inconsistency or intentional stalling on the part of the leader causes additional frustration to those who want to see meaningful, positive change.

This also applies to your customers. Accepting situations when your organization let them down, followed by a swift, heartfelt apology, goes a long way. An outstanding example is Zoom, the communications technology company based in California. At the height of the pandemic, they took ownership of their global security issues and later acknowledged a significant service failure that had impacted millions of customers in the US. Velchamy Sankarlingam, president of product and engineering, took full responsibility by issuing an immediate public statement, which received plaudits from renowned publications and news outlets. In an *Inc.* article, Jason Aten[6] called the company's response an "extraordinary example of emotional intelligence." Sankarlingam's actions not only showed customers that he cared but also demonstrated to employees that accountability is a corporate value for all to uphold.

UNFORTUNATELY, ALL the credibility killers I've mentioned have a negative impact on your culture and relationships at all levels. The Zoom example illustrates that these can be avoided if leaders are open and willing to own their shortcomings. When the inner circle is ready to act boldly and vocalize feedback constructively, then the loss of valued employees and customers, the cost of rehiring, and a decline in morale need not be the inevitable wake-up calls required to restore trust and credibility.

Whether you have been at the helm of your organization for years or have recently embarked on your leadership journey, owning your mistakes is a responsibility that doesn't come easily for most leaders. But demonstrating accountability is a liberating experience. Displays of humility serve as teachable moments. Your team has an opportunity to learn more about accountability when they bear witness to your real-time examples. By walking your talk, you build a powerful culture of accountability without demanding it from others.

Real-Time Takeaways

- Increase your accountability quotient by assessing core leadership attributes such as consistency, humility, trust-building, and dependability.

- Accountability starts and ends with you. Expecting your team members to be accountable means taking ultimate responsibility and modeling the behavior you wish to see in others. When you are the best version of you, that inspires others to offer up the best of themselves.

- Employees have ushered in a new era of self-expression, using social media to voice their opinions on a host of business and social issues. It is incumbent on leaders to demonstrate accountability and respond proactively.

- Be mindful of instant credibility killers that erode your reputation. Acknowledging your mistakes or errors in judgment is often well received and appreciated.

Real-Time Action Step

There is a strong desire for greater accountability, transparency, and exemplary leadership from your employees' vantage point. Regarding your own leadership style, think of an example where there is room for improvement in one of these areas.

THE EVOLUTION OF TALENT MANAGEMENT

"You can no more win a war than you can win an earthquake."

JEANNETTE RANKIN

THE GLOBAL construction industry is a prime example of a strong market sector that continues to experience talent shortages because of misperceptions and inaccurate labeling of the younger generations. The industry is not atypical in this sense and thus serves as a relevant example for all organizations that want to evolve how they manage their talent and gain a competitive edge in doing so.

I have had the pleasure of working with several highly reputable construction firms. Two in particular stood out from the rest, though they could not have been more different. One was led by Ted, a mover and shaker and an entrepreneur who took over the business from his father. The other firm was also a family business, but Bruce, the CEO, was disillusioned and frustrated by the constant grind associated with finding, keeping, and motivating a young workforce. Both Bruce and

Ted recognized that many of their employees were retiring and would need replacing, but good tradespeople were in demand and hard to find. Interestingly, their respective approaches and attitudes toward the young talent pool were in stark contrast.

On the one hand, Bruce described his younger workers as lazy, selfish, and entitled. No surprise that he was getting exactly what he projected: no-shows at his job sites, tardiness, and conflict with other team members. On the other hand, Ted, who mentored his apprentices and newer employees, was rewarded with high productivity, low turnover, and harmonious coworker relationships. Bruce could not see how he was affecting issues he wished to resolve with his attitude. When I asked him what his plans were to address the shortage of talent and manage the attitudinal challenges, he replied, "It is what it is." In addition, when performance issues such as lateness or conflict escalation arose, there were no consequences because his foreman and supervisors did not provide timely feedback.

In contrast, Ted was deeply attuned to the differences in his teams' work and communication styles. He made leadership development a priority for his senior team, foremen, and supervisors, and he made sure the importance of accountability was a clear two-way street. Expectations regarding performance on a job site were established from the outset. If a worker was late more than once, he received a warning from his immediate supervisor. The employee was made aware punctuality was paramount because of his role on the team project. If the problem persisted, the employee was terminated.

The disparity between the CEOs' approaches to their workers was evident in their day-to-day interactions and long-term HR strategies. Bruce was reacting to the prevailing market conditions, while Ted was proactively engaging with his entire workforce, investing heavily in training and team building, and creating a positive environment. It should be obvious which leader is more equipped to lead in real time.

Is the Talent War Over?

Competition for talent has become part of the leadership lexicon as organizations go to extraordinary lengths to attract high-quality employees. Whether you have been in your leadership position for several decades or have recently stepped into your role, talent management should be a top-of-mind priority. The process of attracting, developing, and retaining great people has evolved considerably, and it continues to be a key component of the overall business strategy across numerous industries.

The expression "war for talent" was coined by Steven Hankin of McKinsey & Company in 1997.[1] Since that time, organizations have been obsessed with the battle that began when the demand for highly skilled, sought-after professionals in various disciplines exceeded supply. HR professionals and renowned research firms emphasized the importance of winning the talent war, a challenge that has become more difficult in an ever-changing business environment.

So, is the talent war over? Well, not quite. Although some have proclaimed that the difficult economic times and higher levels of unemployment heralded the end of this so-called battle, I think of the competition for highly skilled workers as ongoing. The complexion of this war keeps changing and, as such, real-time leaders need to adjust simultaneously. We are in the era of freelance work and independent contractors, known as the gig economy (p. 42). This form of contract work has grown exponentially in Europe as well as North America, bringing benefits to both non-salaried workers as well as employers. For leaders of the future, hiring independent contractors will define the future.

The Impact of Recession

Traditionalists, baby boomers, Gen Xers, millennials, and, most recently, Gen Zers have all experienced global recessions and their consequences, specifically, unemployment. During every major economic downturn, people from all generational cohorts have suffered disillusionment, frustration, and angst regarding the effect on their employment prospects and livelihoods. This cycle continues to repeat itself across all generations in the workplace.

In the aftermath of the global financial crisis of late 2007 to mid-2009 and the Great Recession, two significant changes occurred: baby boomers began to retire in greater numbers, and new technologies were in demand and organizations required new skill sets to successfully integrate this technology in their businesses. Millennials answered the call. Equipped with unprecedented capabilities and knowledge, demand for their skills accelerated, outpacing availability of employee supply.

And then Gen Z arrived (not to mention the massive global interruption of the COVID-19 pandemic).

The employment landscape changed drastically during the first quarter of 2020 after WHO declared the pandemic. For Generation Z, this was a decisive moment, as most had not experienced a recession directly. Many G7 countries were experiencing record low unemployment levels prior to COVID-19. With the exception of a handful, almost all were thrust into significant economic downturn and labor market crises. And at the opposite end of the spectrum, the poorest nations, already experiencing excessive financial hardship and extreme unemployment, were hit even harder.

Today, the coexistence of a new talent pool, post-pandemic unpredictability in the global job market, and the ongoing need to transform technologically presents unique challenges for leaders. What are the implications for organizations world-wide around managing their talent? First, bear these points in mind:

1   **Unemployment and underemployment can coexist.** Many employers will still need certain talent that is hard to find. Although research indicates that every demographic will be impacted by the pandemic, there is strong evidence of increased demand for workers in both blue- and white-collar occupations such as IT, manufacturing, engineering, government, healthcare, and an array of supply chain positions. And this demand[2] should accelerate despite economic uncertainty.

2   **The workforce is resilient.** There is no doubt that all sectors of the workforce felt the impact of the 2020 pandemic. Studies show that Gen Z in particular will find it especially difficult and will be bearing the future financial brunt more than other cohorts. Gusto, a payroll service provider in the US, in looking at the real-time impact[3] of the pandemic on small-business employees, noted that workers under the age of twenty-five experienced a rate of layoffs 93 percent higher than that of workers above the age of thirty-five. Nonetheless, Gen Z is a particularly resilient, resourceful, and highly educated demographic who anticipate a bright future for themselves and the planet.

3   **The market will recover.** Although economists don't possess clairvoyance, most would agree based on historical

precedent that there will be a return to brighter days. As noted in Chapter 3, prioritizing talent management is critical in any fiscal environment and especially during a recessionary climate. Insulating your business from forces that are outside of your control includes taking preventative measures to protect your assets and eliminate deficiencies. Your decision to nurture and reward your talent pool during tough times will pay dividends during the next economic upswing.

4   **You still need the right people on the bus, in the right seats.** Jim Collins's apropos "First Who"[4] philosophy—referencing the immortal words of Dick Cooley, ex-CEO of Wells Fargo—has stood the test of time. Collins explained that Cooley intuitively understood what was needed to move his company through the massive deregulation of the banking sector. Cooley explained to his board that he first needed to "get the right people on the bus, the wrong people off the bus, and the right people in the right seats." You need the right people in place before you set the direction. Real-time leaders like Cooley are acutely aware of their industry's challenges and realize that they need the right talent on board in order to respond optimally, as the moment requires.

DESPITE THE ups and downs, the bigger questions remain: As a leader, how resilient are *you*? Are you anticipating the future with confidence, and how are you managing your talent?

Korn Ferry, a global management consulting firm based in California, conducted an in-depth "future-ready" leadership study with far-reaching implications. Its findings confirmed that many leaders are not only ill-equipped to guide their organizations into the future, but they are also ill-prepared to manage the imminent talent crunch.[5]

Your decision to nurture and reward your talent pool during tough times will pay dividends.

Don't Shrink Yourself to Glory

During recent recessionary periods, many organizations understandably looked for ways to cut costs to survive. The first line items to cut are usually advertising, marketing, and hiring. I recall working with the senior leadership of a multinational professional services firm shortly after the Great Recession. During their meeting, the leaders had difficulty achieving consensus regarding their talent attraction and retention strategies. A member of the team aired his concern: we can't shrink ourselves to glory. The group's dilemma was understandable as the potential loss would also have an impact on client retention and profitability.

Fast forward ten years and beyond to a new world of work and must-haves for organizational survival. Human capital remains at the top of the list. How you source that capital will continue to evolve. The real-time decisions you make regarding talent acquisition and retention will have implications for business continuity. Unpredictability and uncertain times are part of the cycle. Making hard choices regarding your workforce comes with the territory. However, the fundamentals, such as treating your talent with dignity and respect, will not change. People remember how their employers dealt with economic downturns. Your organization will still need to advance technologically. Ultimately, you will need talent to fill new, vital positions—maybe more than they need *you*.

By implementing the following solutions, you will be better equipped to help yourself and your organization to be future-ready.

Focus on Your Employer Brand

In their book published almost thirty years ago, Ken Blanchard and Sheldon Bowles described the process of converting customers into "raving fans."[6] But they also noted that having satisfied customers was no longer enough for a business to remain viable. Today, your current and future workforce, in addition to your customers, are also paying close attention to your brand. Your organization's position regarding sustainability, the environment, and a host of social and ethical issues will not go unnoticed. When employees speak positively about their work experience through their own social circles and online networks, they become your cheerleaders and brand ambassadors.

There is nothing more powerful than having your team voluntarily and willingly sharing your brand's story to augment your marketing and HR strategies. This is achieved by articulating your employee value proposition (EVP) or defining the essence of your company—how it is unique and what it stands for. The process begins by brainstorming and collaborating with your employees and leaders to discover why prospective talent would want to work for your organization. Examples of specific questions to help develop your EVP include the following:

- What is it that people want when they come to our organization?

- What is appealing about our business that would attract them into our organization?

- What do our current employees want?

- What do our future employees want?

- Why would they want to continue to work for our organization?

When you are committed to learning more about the values, needs, and desires of your next generation of talent, you will be ideally positioned to create the type of organization that reflects what is important to *them*. For example, the new generation of talent wants flexibility, room to be creative, to be challenged, and, ultimately, to know that what they are doing is making a difference. Increasing your understanding regarding *their* perspectives, career aspirations, and expectations means you will achieve higher levels of success with your talent management strategies.

Build a Sought-After Culture

If you've got your culture right, there is not much that you can't accomplish. Culture is the sum total of the values and beliefs of your workforce. It reflects the personality of your organization. Although culture is intangible, it makes a statement to the world. Ideally, the message to prospective talent reads: this is a great place to work!

Prospective talent will continue being attracted to outstanding workplace cultures. Therefore, it is incumbent on leaders to inspire and engage all team members to be part of an exciting future in a manner that is relevant and meaningful to them. Nothing has more impact on the bottom line success of your company than culture.

Bryan Walker, partner and managing director of IDEO, a multinational design firm, has a great analogy to describe workplace culture: "Culture is like the wind. It is invisible; yet its effect can be seen and felt."[7] Think about how an airplane encounters crosswinds or headwinds. Excessive crosswinds may either ground the aircraft or postpone a landing. Strong headwinds will slow its speed significantly. The environment at your workplace is also vulnerable to adverse "wind conditions." When these types of winds occur, they can throw your plans off course. Your task is to maintain control and navigate your aircraft with intention and purpose.

Every action you take to demonstrate appreciation is a reflection of your culture. Every internal interaction is a reflection of your values. And your values are the essence of your brand's identity. If you want to attract the best and brightest, focus relentlessly on creating the most positive and powerful culture possible.

Prioritize the Employee Experience

Being part of an extraordinary workplace culture creates an exhilarating experience for any team. How employees experience their work and professional interactions is as important as the customer experience. Simply put, your organization needs to execute a clear game plan to ensure that an employee succeeds right from the start. Remove all roadblocks such as vague goals and meaningless platitudes. The process of attracting and recruiting great talent remains a priority, and your goal is to safeguard your investment in your talent with an intentional, well-designed onboarding program (see Chapter 6).

Hire for the Right Fit

Although skills and aptitude are important, attitude and values are equally, if not more, important. There is a direct correlation between culture, turnover, and profitability. If you create a workplace where people *want* to go to work, rather than feeling that they *have* to go to work, you will see tangible results when it comes to your talent retention strategy.

Digitize Talent Management Strategy

Digitization is no longer optional for businesses. This also applies to all aspects of the HR function where the need for data-led initiatives continues to accelerate. HR professionals must be equipped to digitally transform their departments so they can successfully execute talent management strategies. In his article in HR Technologist, author Chiradeep BasuMallick describes the ideal state[8] for HR as follows: "a digital HR strategy [that] will align HR priorities to business outcomes—employee engagement to customer experience, skill-based hiring to productivity, workforce analytics to cost reduction, and more." Your goal as a leader is to support the role of HR and encourage ongoing implementation of digital processes that can add significant overall value to your organizational operations.

Reassess Your Attitude

For employers, the most stressful aspect of talent management is accepting that the process isn't static. Employees' needs are constantly evolving, and you may not be able to meet their unique desires or to retain them. The cost of turnover, especially for skilled workers and senior leadership positions, will continue to rise, not only in terms of replacement and retraining but also the intangible repercussions on your organization and workforce overall, such as disengagement and lower productivity.

Despite these challenges, remember to influence what you can. Is it possible to create the best environment where people can thrive? Absolutely! Can you shift your perspectives regarding the labels you attach to your younger employees? Yes, provided you are willing to do so.

As with many segments of business, factors that are outside of a leader's control, such as government legislation, retirements, and ongoing cost increases, should not be deterrents to growth and future viability. A real-time leader recognizes they need to reassess their attitude, perceptions, and personal biases that negatively impact growth, profitability, and hiring the best people. Although you may not be able to stop your talent from leaving, you can certainly influence their overall experience by creating the best environment while ensuring you are the best version of yourself.

WHEN PEOPLE enjoy their colleagues and work environment, they are less likely to look elsewhere. Plain and simple. Employers that focus on creating the optimum environment and conditions recognize that their prospective talent pool notices everything. This factor alone can be perceived by talent as a significant point of difference as they evaluate their options. Now, and into the future, one thing remains clear in the talent war: a satisfied employee is a happy and productive one. People will continue to buy into the vision and mission of your organization when their efforts are acknowledged, when they know that you are pulling out all stops to provide the best setting for them to succeed.

Ted, the owner of one of the construction firms I talked about at the beginning of this chapter, was successful because he understood that talent was the essential foundation supporting his "structure." He operated in real time by recognizing that the hopes, ambitions, and values of his new workforce didn't need to resemble those of previous teams. Ted differed from the other construction business leader, Bruce, for several key reasons. First, he advocated fairness, respect, and exemplary performance, regardless of age or background. As a result, Ted's company experienced lower turnover because he not only offered an attractive salary and benefits package but also flexible hours and ongoing training opportunities for all workers. The training was entirely funded by the company, as well as regular social and team activities. In Ted's words, "We like hanging out together."

When employees speak well of your business, the process of finding and keeping great people becomes easier.

Real-Time Takeaways

- From the standpoint of today's talent, a company's culture, their brand reputation, and whether they offer a fulfilling work experience remain core motivators. When the real-time leader zeroes in on these intangibles, they dramatically increase the opportunity to attract and retain talent.

- Develop a strong employee value proposition (EVP). Ask your employees for input. Take the time to develop questions that get to the heart of what inspired them to join your organization and why they stay.

- When difficult times arrive, avoid the reactionary choice of downgrading your talent management plans. Real-time leaders consider the future when evaluating immediate requirements.

- Adopt a pragmatic approach to your talent management strategy. As your organizational needs continue to evolve, remain open and flexible, digitize your HR processes, and continually reevaluate your own attitude to the changing workforce.

Real-Time Action Step

While this chapter is fresh in your mind, schedule a specific time on your calendar to chat with a member of your staff whose talents and achievements you admire. Make a concerted effort to discover more about them as a person, as well as learning more about what they enjoy about working in your organization.

CONCLUSION
CONTROL
WHAT YOU CAN

"The future and the present have collided. What we have is the now."

MICHELLE RAY

WHEN I first entered the world of work, I was fourteen years old. My first employers were small business owners who ran a family business, a retail clothing store in Sydney suburbia. They hired me to help out during school vacations and on the occasional weekend. They were hardworking people who taught me a great deal about running a business, how to work well with others, and how to provide exceptional customer service. Many of their clientele were first-generation Australians, just like the owners, who happened to be my parents.

The customer experience in my parents' store was, in a word, entertaining. People who were in the market for a fur coat, evening gown, or confirmation clothes for their children would bring their entire family to the store. Multiple relatives were involved in a buying decision that often took several hours, during which time the customers were well fed. Fresh baclava and Turkish delight were always on offer. A symphony of sounds could be heard at the back of the store—business was done in Greek and Italian, with a smattering of English—as customers shopped for items that weren't exactly what I would call the latest fashion statement.

Cash was king. Although reality TV hadn't been invented yet, watching my father negotiate with half a dozen family members over the price of a dress was better than watching any popular television program of the day. While the term *workplace culture* wasn't part of my vocabulary back then, one could describe the atmosphere as fun and chaotic, never a dull moment. Those were the good times.

Five years earlier, though, our family was at the brink of financial ruin. I still remember a day when I came home to find my father sitting on the couch in our living room, wearing his navy blue robe, pajamas, and slippers. My mother, who had opened a small store located many miles away from our home, was the sole breadwinner. It was the end of a workday, and she had just come home. Without putting down her purse, she went into the kitchen and immediately began preparing dinner. My father sat quietly, staring into space. He had just made the painful decision to close his small clothing factory as it became clear that his business wasn't going to survive. I had never known him to be unemployed before and I will never forget the look of hopelessness on his face.

When all seemed lost, Mr. Dale, our upstairs neighbor, approached my dad with a plan. The two had struck up a wonderful friendship not long after we had moved into our apartment several years earlier. My mother also became great friends with his wife, Jacqueline, a friendship that lasted fifty years. Mr. Dale, or Uncle Tony to me, made an extraordinary gesture to my father. He invited him to become his business partner and together they would transform one of Uncle Tony's stores into a "fashion discount house." Seizing the moment, they embarked on an incredible journey that became a huge success. Several years later, my father bought out Uncle Tony and expanded the number of stores to include my mother's, as well as the one with the delicious offerings of desserts and attire that I described.

My parents were no strangers to hardship. They survived the Holocaust. Most of their family members were murdered in the gas chambers. After the war, they moved to a new country to rebuild their lives, having to learn a new language and adapt to a new culture. They started businesses only to be hit hard again during recessions of the '70s and '80s. Sadly, during yet another downturn of the 1990s, their business did not survive. Not only did they lose their business, but they also lost their home. But through it all, they demonstrated resilience and an astounding capacity to reinvent themselves.

My parents were my first business role models. They had an extraordinary work ethic, took momentous risks, and endured some of the darkest times in recent history. But they never lost sight of how or why their business existed. They took care of their employees, suppliers, and customers. They were relationship-builders who put people first.

I feel grateful that my parents were my first quintessential leaders. Their respective life journeys personified resilience, although the word itself doesn't do true justice to any efforts I've made to describe their experiences. Nonetheless, as we face a post-pandemic world and the next digital revolution, a great deal can be learned from those who have survived significant hardship and a world of uncertainty. Despite the horrors of war, my parents were determined to look toward the future with hope. Most importantly, the example they set serves as a reminder for all leaders, present and future, to focus on what you *can* control.

The challenges my parents faced in business paled in comparison to their final, more personal tests. At the age of seventy-six, my mother fell victim to the cruelty of dementia. My father took on the role of her caregiver at age eighty, rising to the occasion and bearing witness to her demise, in spite of a breaking heart. When the time came that he was no longer able to look after her, he started an unrelenting quest to ensure that she received the best care, despite being told that every nursing home in Sydney had a twelve-month waiting list. It took my father just over two months to do what others had said would take at least a year. The reason he was able to secure a place for my mother to live out the rest of her days was his ability to endear himself to people at every level. He applied every business and life principle that he knew to a situation over which he had very little control and for which he had low expectations.

It's been more than fifteen years since my parents' voices fell silent, but the enormity of their respective losses is still with me. Like many from their generation, my parents overcame tremendous adversity, and I know that their legacy lives on in me. They were truly my greatest mentors, and I believe there will never be another generation like theirs. As leaders, we have much to learn, appreciate, and apply from their timeless legacy. Here are the lessons I learned from their lives that reverberate almost daily for me, and should also for any real-time leader.

Be Prepared to Face Unanticipated Events

If history has taught us anything, it has reminded us to be ready for the unexpected. Doing all you can to prepare yourself and your organization for unforeseen situations will be advantageous when the unpredictable occurs. Adversity, whether it comes without warning in the form of a small hurdle or a large roadblock, is an occupational hazard. But you can be prepared.

Use Optimism and Resilience to Triumph over Difficulties

Unexpected crises illuminate the need for positive leadership. When you weather the storm and maintain an optimistic outlook, you position yourself and your workforce to be able to manage future challenges. You can choose to put your best foot forward, make the best of your situation, and help your team to do the same. We can overcome seemingly impossible challenges by drawing upon our inner resources. Self-directed leadership is essential in the face of ongoing disruptive change and uncertainty. A leader who is able to model resilience and share their experiences of overcoming adversity is poised to make an immediate, significant difference.

Control What You Can

What makes the difference between surviving and thriving is finding the way to control what you can. This is the single most powerful strategy to help you remain future-ready and able to lead in real-time. The *now* is all we know. It's what we have. It's the sum total of present moments and what we choose to do with them that prepares us for the unknown. As you have seen throughout this book, how you decide to frame or reframe your perspective regarding your workforce, the unexpected, or any stumbling block that will invariably present itself is the key to your success. You can choose to take the lead ... and *be* the lead in times of constant change. Let it start and end with *you*.

ACKNOWLEDGMENTS

MY BOOK writing journey with my second leadership book began in late 2018 when I jotted down some ideas about what has changed and what has stayed the same in the world of work and business. Helping leaders to be the best they can be has always been at the core of my work, and in 2019 my feet barely touched the ground as I traveled to speaking engagements in Australia, Europe, the United States, and across Canada. My schedule was both exhilarating and exhausting, so my writing took a back seat. In January 2020, I was ready to fully commit to the writing process and joined a wonderful book writing group led by Helen Wilke, author and book coach extraordinaire. Being in a state of lockdown, not moving from my office for months on end, was the furthest thing on my mind. When the pandemic suddenly struck with full force, there were no more excuses. With the support of Helen and my "partners in writing crime," Patti Pokorchak, Alexandra Bohnet, and Julie Ellis, I forged ahead, determined to reach my goal and finish my book before a milestone birthday in August. I am forever grateful for your support, wisdom, and encouragement.

Several months into the process, it occurred to me that my teachings about leaders remaining relevant, flexible, and open to new ideas applied to *me*. Realizing that the world had forever changed, I found myself questioning not only what lay ahead, but my own identity as a leadership expert and whether or not I had the energy to persevere in the face of so much uncertainty. I developed a deeper affinity with the challenges and struggles my clients faced, wanting to explore them further. I became more intrigued by their passion, ongoing success, and commitment to the well-being of their workforce during a very difficult period.

I am sincerely grateful to Frank Palmer, Aimée Meher-Homji, Brad Eshleman, Michael Campbell, Jackie Norman, Andrew Scott, Jennifer Turliuk, Donald Cooper, and Phoebe Dodds for sharing their extraordinary leadership stories. You are all leading in real time, each and every day. Paul Bledsoe, you are a great role model and I appreciate you. And to all the leaders with whom I have crossed paths personally and professionally, who unknowingly have shaped who I am and helped me define what leadership means to me: you were in my mind and heart as I penned my book, describing your influence and experiences. Without your leadership, I may not have had the guts to start my business more than twenty-five years ago after emigrating from Australia to Canada... and to keep going through the many peaks and valleys associated with being my own boss.

I am fortunate to have an amazing professional network: my speaking colleagues whom I know I can turn to for support, love, and understanding. Eileen McDargh, you are a brilliant, shining light and incredible friend. Karen Jacobsen, you know how to lift me up and inspire me. Nathalie Plamondon-Thomas, I appreciate your positive words and encouragement, always. Joe Calloway, you have been a wonderful mentor and I am so thankful for every conversation. Mark LeBlanc, I have learned so much from you. Michelle Cederberg, for always being my cheerleader. Jody Urquhart, for our many marathon telephone calls. Codi Shewan, for your generosity of spirit in many ways. Rhonda Scharf, Carol Ring, Halina St. James, Ruth Sirman, Bob Gray, Shelle Rose Charvet, Tina Varughese, Lisa Longball Vlooswyk, Jennifer Buchanan, and Leslie Ehm, you have all provided me with strength and faith at the perfect moment.

When I discovered that my publisher, Page Two, was located exactly one block from my home, I knew that working with Trena White and the Page Two team was meant to be. I am so grateful for the guidance and support I have received. My incredible editor, Sarah Brohman, knew exactly how to work with my manuscript to make it the best it could be. Sarah, every interaction with you was such a pleasure. You have an uncanny way of realizing an author's vision as you brilliantly wove the chapters together. I will treasure our time in the editing phase and will always remain a fan. My sincere thanks to Caela Moffet and Elana Dublanko, my project managers, for your patience and thoughtful insights. To Rachel Ironstone, my copy editor; Peter Cocking, my fabulous cover and interior page designer; and Meghan O'Neill—you are a marketing wizard! Thank you all for your exceptional work!

Nora Ayanian, I am so grateful for your proofreading talents!

To my dear friends and family near and far, your love and support means the world to me. Thank goodness for Zoom and the telephone that kept us connected as I approached the finish line. I love you all very much.

And to my husband, Brian. You have patience like no other and I am so fortunate that you are a far better cook than me. You have been my rock, the best sounding board and encourager that a wife... and author could ask for. I am so blessed to be the recipient of your unconditional love and support.

NOTES

Chapter 1: The Real-Time Leader

1   Michele Parmelee, "The Deloitte Global Millennial Survey 2020: Highlights," Deloitte, June 25, 2020, deloitte.com/us/en/insights/ topics/talent/deloitte-millennial-survey.html.

2   Ryan Pendell, "8 Behaviors of the World's Best Managers," Gallup Workplace, December 30, 2019, gallup.com/workplace/272681/ habits-world-best-managers.aspx.

3   Douglas A. Ready, Carol Cohen, David Kiron, and Benjamin Pring, "The New Leadership Playbook for the Digital Age," *MIT Sloan Management Review*, January 21, 2020, sloanreview.mit.edu/ projects/the-new-leadership-playbook-for-the-digital-age.

4   Daniel Goleman, *Working with Emotional Intelligence* (New York: Bantam Dell, 2000).

5   "New YPO Global Pulse Survey on Trust Finds Young Business Leaders View Trust as Critical but Lack Plans on How to Build It with Employees," YPO, January 14, 2020, ypo.org/news/new-ypo- global-pulse-survey-on-trust-finds-young-business-leaders-view- trust-as-critical-but-lack-plans-on-how-to-build-it-with-employees.

Chapter 2: The Workforce Is Changing and So Must You

1   Darren Lee Pullen, "Back to Basics: Electronic Collaboration in the Education Sector," *Handbook of Research on Electronic*

Collaboration and Organizational Synergy, eds. Janet Salmons and Lynn Wilson (Hershey, PA: IGI Global, 2009), doi.org/10.4018/978-1-60566-106-3.ch014.

2   Julia Kagan, "What Is Generation X (Gen X)?" Investopedia, June 22, 2020, investopedia.com/terms/g/generation-x-genx.asp.

3   "Generation Z Statistics," 99firms, 99firms.com/blog/generation-z-statistics/#gref).

4   Lee J. Miller and Wei Lu, "Gen Z Is Set to Outnumber Millennials within a Year," *Bloomberg*, August 20, 2018, bloomberg.com/news/articles/2018-08-20/gen-z-to-outnumber-millennials-within-a-year-demographic-trends.

5   Bernhard Schroeder, "A Majority of Gen Z Aspires to Be Entrepreneurs and Perhaps Delay or Skip College. Why That Might Be a Good Idea," *Forbes*, February 18, 2020, forbes.com/sites/bernhardschroeder/2020/02/18/a-majority-of-gen-z-aspires-to-be-entrepreneurs-and-perhaps-delay-or-skip-college-why-that-might-be-a-good-idea/?sh=21b33a8d5a45.

6   Parmelee, "The Deloitte Global Millennial Survey 2020."

7   Jessica Kriegel, *Unfairly Labeled: How Your Workplace Can Benefit from Ditching Generational Stereotypes* (Hoboken, NJ: Wiley & Sons, 2016).

8   "Global Consumer Trends, COVID-19 Series," Dynata, September 2020, dynata.com/dynata-global-trends-report-special-edition-series-covid-19.

9   Sarah Schmidt, "The Impact of COVID-19 on Millennials and Gen Z Consumers," MarketResearch.com, June 29, 2020, blog.marketresearch.com/the-impact-of-covid-19-on-millennials-and-gen-z-consumers.

10 Parmelee, "The Deloitte Global Millennial Survey 2020."

11 Klaus Schwab, "The Fourth Industrial Revolution: What It Means and How to Respond," *Foreign Affairs*, December 12, 2015, foreignaffairs.com/articles/2015-12-12/fourth-industrial-revolution.

12 Michael Bucy, Adrian Finlayson, Greg Kelly, and Chris Moye, "The 'How' of Transformation," McKinsey & Company, May 9, 2016, mckinsey.com/industries/retail/our-insights/the-how-of-transformation.

13 Jennifer Wells, "Tire Change: How Canadian Tire's New CEO Has Managed a Baptism by Virus," *Globe and Mail*, December 19, 2020,

theglobeandmail.com/business/article-tire-change-how-canadian-tires-new-ceo-has-managed-a-baptism-by-virus/.

14   Steven ZoBell, "Why Digital Transformations Fail: Closing the $900 Billion Hole in Enterprise Strategy," *Forbes*, March 13, 2018, forbes.com/sites/forbestechcouncil/2018/03/13/why-digital-transformations-fail-closing-the-900-billion-hole-in-enterprise-strategy/?sh=6930f8537b8b.

15   Peter Burris, "Digital Transformation: An Analyst's View," GDS, 2016, gdsgroup.com/insights/technology/digital-transformation-analysts-view.

16   Jackie Wiles, "Mobilize Every Function in the Organization for Digitization," Smarter with Gartner, December 3, 2018, gartner.com/smarterwithgartner/mobilize-every-function-in-the-organization-for-digitalization.

17   "7 Examples of Successful Digital Transformation in Business," Gamelearn, game-learn.com/7-examples-of-successful-digital-transformation-in-business.

18   Alison DeNisco Rayome, "Report: 56% of CEOs Say Digital Transformation Has Increased Profits," TechRepublic, April 24, 2017, techrepublic.com/article/report-56-of-ceos-say-digital-transformation-has-increased-profits.

19   "Meet Your Newest Coworker, a Cobot," Dell Technologies, July 1, 2019, delltechnologies.com/en-us/perspectives/meet-your-newest-coworker-a-cobot.

20   Ryan Jenkins, "8 Ways the Crisis Will Forever Change the Future Workforce," *Entrepreneur*, May 12, 2020, entrepreneur.com/article/350089.

21   "The Global Learner Survey, September 2019," Pearson, pearson.com/content/dam/one-dot-com/one-dot-com/global/Files/news/gls/Pearson_Global_Learner_Survey_2019.pdf.

22   Shelly Steward, "Five Myths about the Gig Economy," *Washington Post*, April 24, 2020, washingtonpost.com/outlook/five-myths/five-myths-about-the-gig-economy/2020/04/24/852023e4-8577-11ea-ae26-989cfce1c7c7_story.html.

23   Mary Baker, "9 Future of Work Trends Post-COVID-19," Smarter with Gartner, June 8, 2020, gartner.com/smarterwithgartner/9-future-of-work-trends-post-covid-19.

24 Lydia Dishman, "No, Remote Work Isn't a 'New' Perk—It's Been Around for about 1.4 Million Years," *Fast Company*, April 16, 2016, fastcompany.com/90330393/the-surprising-history-of-working-from-home.

25 "State of Remote Work: 2020 COVID Edition," Global Workplace Analytics and Owl Labs report, owllabs.com/state-of-remote-work/2020.

26 Jena McGregor, "Hot New Job Title in a Pandemic: 'Head of Remote Work,'" *Washington Post*, September 9, 2020, washington post.com/business/2020/09/09/head-of-remote-work-jobs.

27 Darren Murph, "The Remote Playbook," GitLab, 2021, about.gitlab .com/resources/downloads/ebook-remote-playbook.pdf.

28 Sharon Steel, "The Hottest New Title in Tech: Head of Remote Work," The Org, December 14, 2020, theorg.com/insights/the-hottest-new-title-in-tech-head-of-remote-work.

29 Joe Castaldo, "Chief Remote Working Officers Are Now Navigating Organizations into a Post-pandemic World," *Globe and Mail*, December 18, 2020, theglobeandmail.com/business/article-chief-remote-working-officers-are-now-navigating-organizations-into-a.

30 Gina Narcisi, "5 Hot New-Collar Job Skills for a Post-COVID-19 World," CRN, May 21, 2020, crn.com/slide-shows/security/5-hot-new-collar-jobs-skills-for-a-post-covid-19-world.

31 Nelson D. Schwartz, "New Hope for White-Collar Job Seekers? It Depends on the Job," *New York Times*, June 24, 2020, nytimes .com/2020/06/21/business/economy/coronavirus-job-hunting.html.

32 Cheryl Carleton, "Replacing Workers after COVID-19 Is Going to Come with a High Cost for Everyone," *Fast Company*, April 23, 2020, fastcompany.com/90494319/replacing-workers-after-covid-19-is-going-to-come-with-a-high-cost.

33 Joanna Pachner, "Aritzia's Jennifer Wong Built a Fashion Empire by Leading with Style—and Plenty of Substance," *Globe and Mail*, October 29, 2020, theglobeandmail.com/business/rob-magazine/article-aritzias-jennifer-wong-built-a-fashion-empire-by-leading-with-style/.

34 Homayoun Hatami, Pal Erik Sjatil, and Kevin Sneader, "The Toughest Leadership Test," McKinsey & Company, May 28, 2020, mckinsey.com/featured-insights/leadership/the-toughest-leadership-test.

Chapter 3: Real-Time Leaders Are Ready and Relevant

1   Peter Cappelli, "Spotlight on Recruiting: Your Approach to Hiring Is All Wrong," Business Day, May 17, 2019, businessday.ng/hbr/article/spotlight-on-recruiting-your-approach-to-hiring-is-all-wrong.

2   "New National Study Conducted by Ultimate Software Reveals Need for Greater Focus on Manager-Employee Relationships," press release, December 4, 2017, ultimatesoftware.com/PR/Press-Release/New-National-Study-Conducted-by-Ultimate-Software-Reveals-Need-for-Greater-Focus-on-Manager-Employee-Relationships.

Chapter 4: The Human Factor

1   "What's the #1 Leadership Skill for Overall Success?" PR Wire, March 6, 2016, prwire.com.au/pr/58204/what-s-the-1-leadership-skill-for-overall-success.

2   Becky Frankiewicz and Tomas Chamorro-Premuzic, "Digital Transformation Is about Talent, Not Technology," *Harvard Business Review*, May 6, 2020, hbr.org/2020/05/digital-transformation-is-about-talent-not-technology.

3   Andy Hertzfeld, "Pirate Flag," Folklore, August 1983, folklore.org/StoryView.py?project=Macintosh&story=Pirate_Flag.txt.

4   "The True Cost of a Bad Boss," OnlineMBA, October 14, 2020, onlinemba.com/blog/true-cost-bad-boss.

Chapter 5: Leadership Strategy Is Business Strategy

1   Patrick Mieritz, Gallup Workplace Webinar, January 14, 2021.

2   "The Next Era of Human-Machine Partnerships: Emerging Technologies' Impact on Society & Work in 2030," Institute for the Future for Dell Technologies, report, 2017, delltechnologies.com/content/dam/delltechnologies/assets/perspectives/2030/pdf/SR1940_IFTFforDellTechnologies_Human-Machine_070517_readerhigh-res.pdf.

3   "Employee Training Is Worth the Investment," go2HR (Copyright © 2020 go2 Tourism HR Society. All Rights Reserved. Republished

under license), go2hr.ca/training-development/employee-training-is-worth-the-investment.

4   Leading Effectively staff, "Linking Business Strategy and Leadership Strategy for Better Business Outcome," Center for Creative Leadership, June 25, 2020, ccl.org/articles/leading-effectively-articles/leadership-effectiveness-business-strategy.

5   "The Anxious Optimist in the Corner Office," PwC's 21st CEO Survey, 2018, pwc.com/gx/en/ceo-survey/2018/pwc-ceo-survey-report-2018.pdf.

6   "2019 Global Workforce Transformation Trends Study," Lee Hecht Harrison, 2019, info.lhh.com/workforce-transformation.

7   Stefanie K. Johnson, Ksenia Keplinger, Jessica F. Kirk, and Liza Barnes, "Has Sexual Harassment at Work Decreased Since #Me Too?" *Harvard Business Review*, July 18, 2019, hbr.org/2019/07/has-sexual-harassment-at-work-decreased-since-metoo.

8   "The Power of Parity: How Advancing Women's Equality Can Add $12 Trillion to Global Growth," McKinsey Global Institute, report, September 2015, mckinsey.com/featured-insights/employment-and-growth/how-advancing-womens-equality-can-add-12-trillion-to-global-growth.

9   "Randstad US Survey Reiterates Need for Top-Down Commitment to Gender Equality and Inclusion in Today's Workplace," Randstad, press release, March 6, 2018, rlc.randstadusa.com/press-room/press-releases/randstad-us-survey-reiterates-need-for-top-down-commitment-to-gender-equality-and-inclusion-in-todays-workplace.

10 Cheyna Brower and Nate Dvorak, "Why Employees Are Fed Up with Feedback," Gallup Workplace, October 11, 2019, gallup.com/workplace/267251/why-employees-fed-feedback.aspx.

11 Karyn Twaronite, "A Global Survey on the Ambiguous State of Employee Trust," *Harvard Business Review*, July 22, 2016, hbr.org/2016/07/a-global-survey-on-the-ambiguous-state-of-employee-trust.

12 "Projected Population by Generation: Millennials Overtake Baby Boomers as America's Largest Generation," Pew Research Center, April 28, 2020, pewresearch.org/fact-tank/2020/04/28/millennials-overtake-baby-boomers-as-americas-largest-generation/ft_20-04-27_generationsize_1.

13   Laura Baker, "How to Give the Right Amount of Feedback to High
     Performers," February 14, 2017, ClearCompany, blog.clearcompany
     .com/how-to-give-the-right-amount-of-feedback-to-high-performers.

Chapter 6: Engagement Is Evergreen

1   Andy Burjek, "Re-engaging with William Kahn 25 Years after He
    Coined Term Employee Engagement," December 14, 2015, Work
    force.com. workforce.com/news/re-engaging-with-william-kahn-
    25-years-after-he-coined-term-employee-engagement.

2   Jim Harter, "Historic Drop in Employee Engagement Follows
    Record Rise," Gallup Workplace, July 2, 2020, gallup.com/work
    place/313313/historic-drop-employee-engagement-follows-record-
    rise.aspx.

3   "Korn Ferry Survey: 90 Percent of Executives Say New Hire Reten-
    tion an Issue," Korn Ferry, press release, March 21, 2017, kornferry
    .com/about-us/press/korn-ferry-Korn-Ferry-survey-90-percent-of-
    executives-say-new-hire-retention-an-issue.

4   "Benefits of Using Qualitative Research within Your Employee
    Engagement Surveys," Edgecumbe, edgecumbe.co.uk/benefits-
    of-using-qualitative-research-within-your-employee-engagement-
    surveys.

5   "Reverse Mentoring—What Is It, and Does Your Company Need It?"
    Chapple, January 13, 2020, chapple.ltd.uk/2020/01/13/reverse-
    mentoring-what-is-it-and-does-your-company-need-it.

6   "CEOx1Day: About the Program," Odgers Berndtson, odgersberndt
    son.com/en-ca/ceox1day/about-the-program.

7   "25 Leadership Skills You Need to Learn Fast," IMD, imd.org/imd-
    reflections/leadership-reflections/leadership-skills/.

Chapter 7: Meaning Is the New Motivation

1   David Lancefield, "How to Get Your Company's People Invested
    in Transformation," *Strategy+Business*, April 4, 2019, strategy-
    business.com/blog/How-to-get-your-companys-people-invested-
    in-transformation.

2   Alan Kohll, "How One Company Is Taking Care of Employees during Covid-19," *Forbes*, April 6, 2020, forbes.com/sites/alankohll/ 2020/04/06/how-one-company-is-taking-care-of-employees-during-covid-19.

3   Parmelee, "The Deloitte Global Millennial Survey 2020."

4   Parmelee, "The Deloitte Global Millennial Survey 2020."

5   Tammy Erickson, "Meaning Is the New Money," *Harvard Business Review*, March 23, 2011, hbr.org/2011/03/challenging-our-deeply-held-as.

Chapter 8: Voices Rising

1   "Amazon Co-founds the Climate Pledge, Setting Goal to Meet the Paris Agreement 10 Years Early" Amazon, press release, September 19, 2019, press.aboutamazon.com/news-releases/news-release-details/amazon-co-founds-climate-pledge-setting-goal-meet-paris.

2   Abel Gustafson, Anthony Leiserowitz, and Edward Maibach, "Americans Are Increasingly 'Alarmed' about Global Warming," Yale Program on Climate Change Communication, February 12, 2019, climatecommunication.yale.edu/publications/americans-are-increasingly-alarmed-about-global-warming.

3   "The New World of Work: Report Warns of an Unprecedented Rise in Workplace Activism," Herbert Smith Freehills, November 25, 2019, herbertsmithfreehills.com/latest-thinking/the-new-world-of-work-report-warns-of-an-unprecedented-rise-in-workplace-activism-v2.

4   Michael Bloomberg, "Message from Mike," in Bloomberg Impact Report 2019, page 3, data.bloomberglp.com/company/sites/56/ 2020/05/Impact-Report-2019d.pdf#page=3.

5   Colin Lecher, "Google Employees 'Refuse to Be Complicit' in Border Agency Cloud Contract," The Verge, August 14, 2019, theverge.com/2019/8/14/20805432/google-employees-petition-protest-customs-border-cloud-computing-contract.

6   Kirsten Herhold, "How Businesses Are Responding to the Death of George Floyd and the Resulting Protests," Clutch, June 10, 2020, clutch.co/hr/resources/how-businesses-are-responding-george-floyd-death-resulting-protests.

7   Aaron Foley, "America's Great Racial Reckoning Comes to the Auto Industry as Some Ford Employees Call for End of Cop Car Manu-

facturing," Jalopnik, August 7, 2020, jalopnik.com/america-s-great-racial-reckoning-comes-to-the-auto-indu-1844285290.

8   Alex Hern and Julia Carrie Wong, "Facebook Employees Hold Virtual Walkout over Mark Zuckerberg's Refusal to Act Against Trump," *The Guardian*, June 1, 2020, theguardian.com/tech nology/2020/jun/01/facebook-workers-rebel-mark-zuckerberg-donald-trump.

9   Selena Simmons-Duffin and Pien Huang, "CDC Employees Call Out Agency's 'Toxic Culture of Racial Aggressions,'" NPR, July 13, 2020, npr.org/sections/health-shots/2020/07/1⅜89769017/cdc-employees-call-out-agencys-toxic-culture-of-racial-aggression.

10 Whitney Bauck, "Refinery29 Founder Christene Barberich Steps Down as Editor-In-Chief in Response to Accusations of Racism and Toxic Company Culture," Fashionista, June 8, 2020, fashionista.com/2020/06/christene-barberich-refinery29-racism.

11 Ian Shugart, "Call to Action on Anti-racism, Equity, and Inclusion in the Federal Public Service," Privy Council Office of the Government of Canada, press release, January 22, 2021, canada.ca/en/privy-council/corporate/clerk/call-to-action-anti-racism-equity-inclusion-federal-public-service.html.

12 Gerry Smith, "Bleacher Report CEO Steps Down amid Staff Diversity Concerns," BNN Bloomberg, June 23, 2020, bnnbloomberg.ca/bleacher-report-ceo-steps-down-amid-staff-diversity-concerns-1.1455125.

Chapter 9: The Demand for Accountability

1   Dominic-Madori Davis, "7 Slang Words Gen Zers Coined in the Coronavirus Era, and What They Actually Mean," *Business Insider*, April 8, 2020, businessinsider.com/slang-gen-z-made-to-describe-coronavirus-pandemic-2020-4.

2   Baker, "9 Future of Work Trends Post-COVID-19."

3   "The Importance of Honesty and Integrity in Business," Brian Tracy International, briantracy.com/blog/leadership-success/importance-of-honesty-integrity-in-business.

4   Edgar H. Schein and Peter A. Schein, *Humble Leadership: The Power of Relationships, Openness, and Trust* (Oakland, CA: Berrett-Koehler, 2018).

5   John Hamm, "The Five Messages Leaders Must Manage," *Harvard Business Review*, May 2006, hbr.org/2006/05/the-five-messages-leaders-must-manage.

6   Jason Aten, "Zoom Just Failed Its Biggest Test. Its Apology Is an Extraordinary Example of Emotional Intelligence," *Inc.*, August 25, 2020, inc.com/jason-aten/zoom-just-failed-its-biggest-test-its-apology-is-an-extraordinary-example-of-emotional-intelligence.html

Chapter 10: The Evolution of Talent Management

1   Scott Keller and Mary Meaney, "Attracting and Retaining the Right Talent," McKinsey & Company, November 24, 2017, mckinsey.com/business-functions/organization/our-insights/attracting-and-retaining-the-right-talent.

2   Ben Jay, "8 In-Demand Jobs for the Postcoronavirus Economy That Can Pay as Much as $136,000," Grow, May 6, 2020, grow.acorns.com/in-demand-jobs-post-coronavirus-economy/.

3   Daniel Sternberg, "The Real-Time Impact of COVID-19 on Small Business Employees," Gusto, May 1, 2020, gusto.com/company-news/smb-employee-covid-19-impact.

4   Jim Collins, "First Who... Then What," in *Good to Great: Why Some Companies Make the Leap... and Others Don't* (New York: HarperCollins, 2001), 44–45.

5   Michael Distefano, "Introducing: A New Breed of Future-Ready Leaders," Focus, 2018, focus.kornferry.com/leadership-and-talent/introducing-a-new-breed-of-future-ready-leaders.

6   Ken Blanchard and Sheldon Bowles, *Raving Fans: A Revolutionary Approach to Customer Service* (New York: HarperCollins, 1993).

7   Jason Portnoy, "Culture Matters," Oakhouse Partners, September 26, 2018, medium.com/oakhousevc/culture-matters-97ca0f0282c1.

8   Chiradeep BasuMallick, "Building a Digital HR Strategy? Here's Everything You Need to Know," HR Technologist, April 26, 2019, hrtechnologist.com/articles/hr-analytics/tips-to-build-a-digital-hr-strategy.

INDEX

ABOUT
THE AUTHOR

HOW MANY people can identify with a predominantly negative leadership experience early in their careers? That was how Michelle Ray's foray into the world of work began after she excitedly accepted a position in the media advertising industry while still living in Sydney, Australia. Though she heard, "You will never make it as a manager,"  Michelle ignored her critical, misogynistic boss and worked her way up the leadership ladder, devoid of role models or mentors. By increasing sales revenues of twenty-five leading Australian radio and television affiliate stations, Michelle helped generate record-breaking revenues for the sales team of the world's largest cinema advertising contractor during a severe recessionary climate.

With a proven background in achieving outstanding results as a business leader, Michelle was inspired to help leaders engage more meaningfully with their teams and create dynamic workplace cultures. She established her speaking, leadership training, and consulting business in 1995, shortly after immigrating to Vancouver, Canada. Michelle has since worked as an in-demand keynote speaker and respected thought leader for an array of renowned brands, government organizations, and diverse industry associations around the world.

In addition to her corporate background, Michelle broadened her leadership experience during her tenure as a program director with the nonprofit Junior Achievement. She secured financial commitments and volunteer support from numerous corporations, facilitating enduring partnerships between youth, entrepreneurs, and educators that helped teach future generations about business.

Michelle is the author of *Lead Yourself First! Indispensable Lessons in Business and in Life*. She is also a Certified Speaking Professional, the highest designation in the speaking industry's international measure of professional platform skills.

When not on the road, Michelle loves watching as many NHL games as possible, exploring the mountains of British Columbia, and spending time with her grandchildren.

michelleray.com
realtimeleadership.com

Bring Michelle Ray
and *Leading in Real Time*
to Your Organization

Keynotes and Leadership Training

Hire Michelle for your next virtual or in-person conference, meeting, or professional development retreat and experience her powerful, dynamic, and engaging presentation style. On stage or online, Michelle will captivate, educate, and energize your leadership and management teams with practical and actionable strategies that you'll be applying long after your event ends. Michelle will work with you to create a customized, highly enjoyable, and memorable session, packed with stories and content to shift perspectives and help your leadership group hone essential skills for maximum results.

On-Demand Learning Programs

Michelle's Real Time Leadership Academy provides leaders and teams with an array of on-demand workshops and presentations, covering topics that include *Leading in Real Time*, *Leadership Starts with Me*, *Who Moved My Future? Demystifying the Fear of Change*, *Retain the Best & Confront the Rest*, *Leading Remote Teams*, and *Success Strategies for Resilient Leadership*.

Bulk Book Orders

Take advantage of special pricing for bulk book purchases to provide copies of *Leading in Real Time* for your entire leadership team.

Find out more about Michelle's services, her Real Time Leadership Academy, and bulk book orders by contacting michelle@ michelleray.com.

michelleray.com
realtimeleadership.com